I AM ON MY WAY TO HEALING

I AM ON MY WAY TO HEALING

Two Strokes and a Recovery

Robert P. Parker, PhD

I AM ON MY WAY TO HEALING
TWO STROKES AND A RECOVERY

iUniverse books may be ordered through booksellers or by contacting:

iUniverse
1663 Liberty Drive
Bloomington, IN 47403
www.iuniverse.com
1-800-Authors (1-800-288-4677)

ISBN: 978-1-4917-7560-8 (sc)
ISBN: 978-1-4917-7561-5 (e)

Library of Congress Control Number: 2015914471

Print information available on the last page.

iUniverse rev. date: 10/16/2015

TABLE OF CONTENTS

PART IV
Road To Healing

PART V
Increasing Moments Of Understanding

Dedicated to my wife of thirty-four years, Josephine Cleonice Mazzoli: you are my friend, partner for life, and caregiver – and beyond!

Jo, you were the first one to see anything that I had written post-stroke. This event was before the first page was even finished. It all seemed to go nowhere. Just all bits and pieces, and some of them didn't make any sense to me. But, you said, "This a start! Keep it going." I finally did, and this book is the result. You were in at the beginning and at the end. Kudos!

PREFACE

In this book Bob Parker gives an account of his experience of a devastating stroke and ongoing recovery. The events track back to December 2009, and the story goes on from here. It's a fascinating and instructive read. Bob – Dr. Robert P. Parker – is a scholar. His discipline is the English language, its nature and acquisition. As a professor of English Education in the Graduate School of Education at Rutgers University, Bob taught teachers about language learning and learning language. The stroke left Bob without language and without thought. Where they went, language and thought, and how they came back are a big part of his story – rather, for me, they are his story.

As I've connected with Bob at various stages of his recovery, what's most noticeable is the re-emergence in something like the "same old," but with a difference. Certainly, he's just about the same, but arguably, maybe in some ways, better. He knows a lot more now about language, learning, memory, voice, and himself – and their interdependence. It really is his first choice of a subject for investigation – himself – but he really does make his disciplined focus on day to day recovery work as scholarship, story telling and recovery. Or character expansion. As the story goes on, Bob is getting back to Bob, with a difference. Sort of the same, arguably better.

The book is a good read. At once, inspirational and instructive – cast with all the ingredients of a good story: solid characterization, deft dialogue, an anticlimax as prologue, multiple valuable insights about trauma and recovery and always -- well wrought suspense.

Peter D. Brown
Orillia, Ontario, Canada

INTRODUCTION

I worked for fifty years as an educator/administrator in high schools, in community colleges, in universities, and as a director and a consultant. At the beginning of my educational career, I received a Bachelor's degree (English) from Williams College in 1959 and a Master of Arts in Teaching degree (English Education) from Johns Hopkins University in 1960. Then I moved to Illinois where I taught at New Trier High School, at Northwestern University (where I got my Ph.D.), and at the University of Chicago. But after ten years of teaching in Chicago, in one high school and two major universities, I took a job teaching doctoral students at Rutgers University in New Jersey. During the twenty years that I spent at Rutgers, I spent a year at the University of London (1975-1976), a year In Italy (1981-1982), and two years at Sheridan College in Ontario, Canada (1987-1989).

After twenty years, I "retired" from Rutgers, but not from teaching and/or educational administration. Because my wife, Jo, and I decided to make a major change to a drier climate and a more moderate temperature, we moved all the way west to Reno, Nevada. I thought that I would be hired immediately at the University of Nevada-Reno. But each time that I applied, I wasn't even given the courtesy of an interview. There were jobs in Reno for insiders in English Education and in other fields, but not for me as an outsider trying to break in. With my background, my knowledge, my skills, and my list of publications, I was easily marketable for the East Coast but, apparently, not for the West Coast. So, after eight and a half years floundering around looking for a job, and finding one that I liked but didn't pay enough money, I gave up the search in Reno and applied for a job in Las Vegas, five hundred miles to the south.

Hired immediately in Las Vegas, I spent the next four years as a coordinator of grants administration with the Clark County School District, the fifth largest school district in the country. With the subsequent job, as coordinator of research and development, it was great for a while, but then went downhill fast. So, after eight and a half years with the school district, I "retired" again. I immediately moved into a new job with a private educational company located in Boulder City, Nevada. Don, the owner of the Delphi Company, provided me with a variety of consulting contracts, and I also picked up some contracts for myself. The people, including Don, I worked with were superior, both creatively and innovatively. However, after four years of successful employment, Jo and I decided to move to Pasadena, California, in order to take advantage of living at a lower altitude and in a warmer climate than in Las Vegas (2,600 feet versus 700 feet).

So, searching exclusively online, I applied for a couple of different jobs. This position, though, was the only one I received that I was excited about. It was at the University of La Verne, California, and, miraculously, I got the job that I wanted at 71 years of age. This time I moved back to the graduate university with doctoral students to boot, with the prospects of teaching and researching in a different kind of environment. I was excited by what lay ahead, but unfortunately, after only one year in the job, I was done in by two strokes.

The real story begins there at the age of 72. I suffered two strokes that affected the use of my right arm, of my right hand, and of my right leg (about 60%), but the worst effect was to my ability to speak. The stroke had left me with expressive aphasia. I was flat on my back in bed and unable to do anything, especially not to utter a sound. I heard five noises! **I could understand what was said to me, but I could not speak at all. So, in the months that followed, I had to learn how to sit up again; I had to learn how to stand up again; and, then, I had to learn how to walk again. I had to train my arm, my hand, and my leg until they worked. But, most importantly, I had to learn how to speak English again for the second time in my career.**

I developed into a professor of radical constructivism and was committed to my beliefs and to my actions that were increasingly synchronized. I published five books and thirty-five articles. Then, after two strokes, I had to learn how to walk by myself, how to move my arm and hand by itself, and how to speak by myself. From the absolute beginning, I struggled to pronounce my first word with the help of Amy, my speech therapist. After about three weeks, I learned how to say an "I". I forced it out between breaths, and I spoke ever so slowly to say "I." I garbled them all up, but, nonetheless, it was a great victory for me. I spoke again, as opposed to not ever speaking permanently, although it was only Amy and Jo who could understand the garbled mess at the beginning.

It may be hard for you to believe, but you can say this phrase or that sentence, speaking quickly in the present moment and, also, thinking ahead of what you are going to say next. In fact, you are thinking well ahead of your actual speaking. **But this was the only word I knew then**! In the very next lesson, I now had to say "I could" or "I could not". I had to learn to speak them once again. My vocabulary had expanded to three complete words. So I could say "I," "I could" and "I could not," but I could not finish any of them past the first beginning of the sentence. The rest of the blanks that came toward the end of the sentence were aphasia-related. But slowly, painfully, stressfully, quite the opposite of quickly, the rest of the words – one by one -- did follow over time, gradually cutting down on the number of blanks I had to fill in.

Now I can write much better than I can speak. So, when you read my writing, rather than hear me speak to you, which is sometimes garbled and sometimes blank, you are "listening" to the voice I want you to hear, which is clear and consistent. You can hear my speaking to you, but you can read my writing that is even more precise, in detail, and longer. And I want you to see how much progress I have to report, in writing especially but also in speaking. In three and a half years, I am on my feet and moving fairly quickly, engaging in social conversation, practicing Tai Chi three times per week, doing the treadmill or swimming two or three times a week, reading fiction, nonfiction, drama, and poetry, writing feelings, thoughts, and ideas about the inner world and about certain aspects of the outer world, listening to music, primarily classical, jazz, and soft rock, and enjoying my art and photography collection. I will probably write a sequel to this book, beginning in the next one or two years. And there is much more to come in the near future!

PART I
WHEN THINGS WERE DIFFERENT

A BRIEF HISTORY

I was born in Somerville, New Jersey, on August 26, 1937. I was the oldest of three brothers. At the beginning of ninth grade, when I entered Somerville High School, I had grown to 5 feet 3 inches and weighed 115 pounds. As a result, I was the last person chosen for each of the sports teams: football, basketball, and baseball. I did, in fact, get to play baseball, but I wasn't able to play in the other two sports. I only played them in practice sessions. I gave up football at the end of ninth grade, although I continued with basketball and baseball. But, between the ninth and tenth grades, I grew amazingly to 6 feet, and I weighed 135 pounds.

I loved basketball! I liked baseball, but not nearly as much as basketball. I liked passing the ball, dribbling back and forth, but especially loved shooting the set shot, the jump shot, and the layup. In my junior year, I'd really taken off making one-hand jump shots (two college players, at the same time, had invented the one-hand jump shot only a year before) and two-hand set shots. Since I was only 135 pounds, the basketball coach "assigned" me a partner. Tony got into every opponent's face, and I continued to score.

At Williams College, I continued playing basketball and baseball and majored in English. After my freshman year, I began to study harder, and my grades slowly improved: all C's in the freshman year, all C's and B's in the sophomore year, and some A's, though more B's, in my junior and senior years. My grades in English especially showed significant improvement over the four years. However, while I was traveling all over Europe with a friend for two months, between my junior and senior years, I sensed a "shift" coming within me. I couldn't have articulated it then, but the two sports that I had been good at, especially basketball, slowly, over the next few years, lost interest for me. That summer, I turned away from sports and sporting events toward books, both nonfiction, fiction, and articles, and I haven't ever looked back.

After graduating from Williams College, I went to graduate school at John Hopkins University in Baltimore for a full year, and I then took a job teaching English at New Trier High School in a suburb of Chicago. My first year there, I began coaching basketball, and I continued for five years. In my second year there, I taught three 10th grade English classes. Not at the beginning of the year, but close to it, in a moment of inspiration, I proposed that the class do a daily series of assignments for a journal writing class. This assignment wasn't part of the 10th grade curriculum or any other curriculum. It was truly an "add-on." It was about a month before I had realized the combination, in writing and in reading, that I had achieved alone. Reading <> journaling <> writing: it was the link between the two topics. And that was before any of the English teachers even became aware of the value of journaling, let alone any others among all the teachers of other subjects at that school or in any other schools. It was a great insight for me as an English teacher and an outstanding personal moment. I had created it by myself!

After I left New Trier, I went to Northwestern University as a full-time doctoral student. After two years, with my Ph.D. in English Education just behind me, I began teaching at the University of Chicago. I had two good years there, but then I moved on to Rutgers University for the next 20 years. Once again I included journal writing in my classes.

After six years of teaching at Rutgers University, I met Jo. I was 39, and Jo was 35. Divorced in 1978, I had two children, Christopher and Jennifer. A short time later, Jo and I moved in together and later got married. Jo and I lived in a variety of places, and we traveled everywhere together. Jo was a friend and a partner for life. She was connected to me intimately, and I, to her, in the same way.

Having Chris, my son, live with us was our first major challenge. Jo, Andrea, Jo's daughter, and I agreed that we could help Chris. Chris was highly intelligent and was talented in music, painting, and science. But Chris was also failing all his subjects in the previous high school, and I knew that there was drug use as well. So, we had the builders add a bedroom onto the house for him. Chris moved all his stuff into the bedroom and Rumson, New Jersey, became his home.

We knew Chris had begun to change when he finally put his first load of clothes in the washing machine. He kept waiting for one of us to wash his clothes for him. He would wear his clothes over and over again without washing them, just dropping them on the floor and picking them from where he had dropped them. So we kept his bedroom door closed, but the smell still seeped under the door.

But the day came when Chris did gather up his entire array of clothes into a mound on the floor. He picked up his socks, pants, T-shirts, and underwear, took them downstairs, jammed them into the washing machine as tight as he could fill it, put in the soap, and turned it on. After he finished washing and drying his clothes, he carried them upstairs in a bundle and put them away in his dresser and his closet. It was grueling, but I slowly did make the shift in focus from me to Chris. I finally wanted <u>him</u>, not me, to become whole for the first time in <u>his</u> life. Finally, Chris had begun to grow up, and I, by the way, had too!

By the time he finished high school and reached mid-sophomore year at the University of Montana, Chris had grown up even more successfully. <u>He</u> had enrolled in the parts of the music program that made sense to <u>him</u> and then moved on to take the parts of the art program that made sense to <u>him</u> as well. He also explored the writing curriculum during which he had drafted a short story about his life and about his "death." However, when I was 45 years old, he died of a massive aneurysm in the carotid artery in his mid-brain. Chris was just 20 years old. I was -- we were -- devastated and depressed. I relied totally on Jo. If I didn't have her with me, I don't know what I would have done. I think I would have been close to suicide. Later we were faced with another tragedy of a different kind, but equally as painful. When Jo was 64 years old, her daughter, Andrea, died of a LAM disease. She was 43 years old, and Jo was devastated. Jo relied totally on me this time.

From a very young age, Jo had had a disease called bronchiectasis. This term is the one that most completely identified her current condition. However, all her life she fought with gut, heart and mind: a heart with two internal leaks, one larger than the other. The right lung was the worse one, and the two were down to about 45 per cent of her breathing capacity in each lung. But, nonetheless, Jo first worked hard at teaching, and then, second, at becoming a marriage and family therapist. She also was a great cook, enjoyed concerts, theater, and art galleries, and worked hard by using the treadmill and by using the small free weights. She was determined to carry on to the full extent she could possibly do.

Jo and I built a great life together. She taught for 15 years: in fifth grade, community college, and then high school. When she changed careers, she worked as a marriage and family therapist for more than 30 years. My career for 50 years was in education: some of those years directly in teaching and others directly or indirectly connected with education.

We took a house together, actually many condos and houses together: first in New Jersey, and then in Toronto, in Reno, in Las Vegas, in Pasadena, and, once again, in Las Vegas. We spent a year abroad in England and in Italy, with two years in Toronto. We made more than 36 visits to Europe: traveled all around Italy, including Sicily, but also in England, Wales, France, Belgium, Holland, Denmark, Switzerland, Norway, Finland, Hungary, Germany, Austria, Spain, and Portugal. Jo and I enjoyed all of these adventures, but especially the trips to Italy that we have made by ourselves and with friends. So, here are a few bits and pieces from the "previous" life that Jo and I had together. And it was a great life, too. But now, everything is totally different after I had two strokes. I had to start again from the beginning.

PART II

THE EVENTS WHICH CHANGED MY LIFE

THE FIRST STROKE

With a kiss goodbye to Jo, I left our condo at about 10:00 a.m. on December 22, 2009. After going down to the garage and starting the Volvo, taking a five minute drive, I pulled into the parking lot of the Jones Coffee Roasters. I was going to buy two cups of coffee -- a soy cappuccino and a regular cappuccino -- and then I would return home. Because the parking lot was full, I had to back out and wait for a parking spot. So I put the car into reverse, and the stroke hit me instantly. But I had my foot on the brake somehow, just before, during, and after the stroke, to bring it to a halt. Suddenly, I could not speak or move anything at all. My hearing was muffled. But I still could hear some of the noises and sounds around me. I was frozen but alive, though barely. A woman in a nearby pet store saw me and brought her cell phone with her. She ran to the car, and, when she saw my situation, she called 911 and help was dispatched immediately.

The ambulance took less than five minutes to reach the spot where I was in the parking lot. When the paramedics came over to my car, they began asking me some questions. I was upright. When they finished with the questions, they began moving me slowly out of the car and onto the ground. Now I was lying down. Because my foot was now off the brake, even though the gear was engaged, the car rolled forward to hit the green bumper, although not hard, for it was about one foot from the curb. I couldn't talk at all during that moment, but I was still more or less alert. The voice of the paramedic came through to me as if it were from somewhere else. But despite it being my intention to cooperate with them, it was hard to concentrate on what the appropriate action was. Everything was clear to me in my mind, but at the same time, it was muffled, strange, and confusing to my ears.

After a brief period, the paramedics lifted me onto a medical gurney, strapped me in tight, and loaded me into the ambulance. I was awake, though still confused about everything. The next thing I can remember is speaking to a paramedic, who was sitting down next to me in the ambulance and asking me some further questions. The answers I gave to the paramedic came out half rational – at least to me it made sense -- and half irrational – it was just gobbledygook.

But I had speech of sorts then. After a five minute ride to the Huntington Memorial Hospital, the paramedics took me out of the ambulance, brought me into the critical care unit, and checked me in with the doctors who were on duty that day. The next thing I remember was that I was placed flat in a bed. Then I went in and out of consciousness, but mostly out for about two or three hours.

FLAT IN BED

For the first time after the stroke, I finally opened my eyes. I can't remember at what hour of the day it was, but it most likely was late afternoon. The first thing I can remember were the faces -– Jo (my wife), Jen (my daughter), Sandy (my son-in-law), the nurses -- all facing me, and Jo's hands holding mine (my left one), though I couldn't recall the words yet.

Now it was just after the first stroke had occurred. The memories of recent events were now flowing through my mind, but these were all jumbled up together. What happened to me came and went in large bundles that I couldn't quite make sense of individually. What happened immediately after the stroke was blurry and confusing, and I went in and out of consciousness. I knew sort of when it happened, but then I sort of did not know either. I was awake when the first stroke occurred, and I also knew more or less what happened in the instant it had occurred. But what went by in the first three or four hours afterwards, and what my thoughts about the "meaning" of the experience were to me, I know only from retrospective accounts. I know what had happened then, sort of, but I was only aware of it at that moment in vague terms. It was more confusing to me than not confusing to me. I knew how the stroke had happened in part, or some of it anyway, but not nearly the entire total of it as a stream of consciousness.

I know also that I had been awake through it all – or through most of it anyway. I do know that, somewhat later on, and, though that might have been a short or a long time I don't know for sure, but I know that I was flat in bed and so tired out down to the very core of my being. I couldn't see my face, but I am told that I looked dazed, ashen, wiped out. When I glanced around at the people surrounding me, they looked really tired as well, but they -- Jo, Jen, Sandy and the nurses -- were extremely glad to see me again! I guess they were worried that I wouldn't wake up at all. But I did awaken, and, opening my eyes, I made it "back" to them. It took me a few seconds, though, to locate them and to place them in my "face-to-face" communication. However, I finally managed to focus on the faces – Jo's particularly -- and on the hands. It took me a few seconds, though, to register the glances from Jo, to the nurses, over to Jen and Sandy, and back to Jo again. Now, the picture was getting a little clearer: not much, but somewhat.

The first thing that I can recall was Jo's face – Jo, a few inches from mine, her exhausted face to my now slightly drooping face, and her hands holding mine – the left hand - grasped as tightly and warmly as Jo could. Jo's hands holding my own face expressed an emotional relief at my regaining consciousness. It was a miracle: two faces coming back together -- again! Her face, as I can recall it now, was alive but truly tired out. However, in relation to mine, Jo's was an absolutely radiant face! My exhausted, ashen face and her face, as totally wiped out as mine, just made it seem as if her tired face was holding onto – really holding onto - my careworn and wasted face! Her face, as I remember it now, served as a gorgeous reminder of who she really was and is: passionately committed to the unfailing admiration and hope that she has in me, and that she will always have in me to the very end!

I could see all her memories of me: long before the stroke began and beyond the stroke to the final end. One day I knew I would be fine again, though it would be a long, long way from the beginning to the "end." But I could do it, as Jo imagined it, although I could not see that then. But Jo could! She could see me back from the beginning of the stroke – actually before the stroke had occurred - to the final end of life. Back from being the nearly dead to re-growing into a man: that was Jo's vision and, also, her commitment.

Jo! Those memories of you just flood in: utter fatigue on my part, but also my joyfulness in seeing you for the very first time immediately after the stroke. And noticing, too, that my left hand, not the right one, was the one you held – in both of your hands. Suddenly I couldn't move my right arm at all, which I realized right at that moment. The right arm and hand were totally dead for me.

11

I had the stroke. Yet, I had awakened from it! I found it truly amazing to look at the "old" faces and, at the same time, the "new" faces! They were the same faces, yet they were truly different. When I had gotten into the car to head off to the Jones Coffee Roasters, I had seen you, Jo, just before the first stroke had occurred. But now I was, also, seeing you for the very first time since the first stroke had occurred.

Jo's first words were "Hi" and "Welcome back!" It seems possible that she could have been saying more than that to me, but I couldn't hear all the words. I can remember, though, that she said those incredible things to me! To me! And it was because I could open my eyes and look at Jo, whose face was tearful, and, at the same time, whose face was radiant with relief. I was exhausted, incredibly weak -- my body, my mind, and my spirit -- and totally unable to speak. But it was the real me, whatever there was left of me. Slowly I discovered that I could not <u>speak</u> at all, but I could <u>actually hear</u> some of the words Jo had spoken to <u>me</u> slowly – not all of them, but some of them!

Rolling my head over to my daughter, Jen, and son-in-law, Sandy, I can recall that both spoke to me. I wanted to say to Jen and Sandy, "Hello", but I couldn't. So Jen said, "Hi", and it was a different kind of message with an "Oh my god, you're alive!" Sandy echoed that with, "How are you doing?" as if he was awfully glad that I was alive. And I was looking around the room to see all of the faces who were there waiting for me, and I had brought them to "life" by slowly opening my eyes.

I was flat on my back, my right arm paralyzed, my right leg a little paralyzed but not as much as the right arm, and my voice completely muted, silent. I was just rolling my head from one side to the other. That was all I could do. I could recognize the concepts and words coming in, the recurring <u>input</u>, or at least most of those words, but I didn't know what the concepts or the words were that needed to go out, the <u>output.</u> I could recognize more than one word, the input, but I just did not hear a single word from the output side! The words <u>coming in</u> made a little bit of sense. I was "aware" of the words coming in. However, I couldn't recognize the words <u>going out</u>! Not just words and voices, but I was totally without sound and speech. I could hear only noises. It would not be until the speech therapist, Amy, gave language back to me that I could communicate once again. But, without the language and without the arm, at that moment, I was completely down, done in. This was the worst situation that I could possibly imagine: not speaking a word of English, flat on my back, with an arm and a hand dead.

DATE OF CONSULTATION: 12/22/2009

REASON FOR CONSULTATION: Code stroke

HISTORY OF PRESENT ILLNESS: The patient is a 72-year-old right-handed gentleman . . . who was brought in by the paramedics after being involved in a motor vehicle accident. I spoke to the patient's wife who reports that he was last known well at 10:00 a.m. when he left the house to go to Jones Coffee House. At 10:00 a.m., he was speaking, moving all his extremities, and without any problems. At approximately 10:30 a.m., he was involved in minor motor vehicle accident at which the paramedics were called. The dispatch was recorded at 10:34 a.m. He was brought to the Huntington Memorial Hospital where a code stroke was activated at 10:56 a.m. I immediately met the patient in the CT scanner where he underwent a CT scan as well as a CT angiogram and CT perfusion. After reviewing the study with Dr. William Wortman, neuroradiologist, it was determined that he had an area of likely watershed infarction, though was less than one third of the middle cerebral artery territory. Also at the time he was noted to have an NIH Stroke Scale of 16, therefore, full-dose t-PA was initiated at 11:30 a.m. I also contacted the patient's primary care physician, Dr. Paulette Saddler, who has recently begun taking care of the patient who has moved here from Las Vegas 6 months ago . . . I also contacted Dr. Mayer Rashtian to evaluate the patient while he was in the hospital. Additionally, I spoke with Dr. Ashish Patel of critical care to help consult on the patient. **At that point, he received 1 point for mild right facial droop as a well as moderate expressive aphasia. His motor function was normal at the time. I had an extensive discussion with the patient's wife as well as with his daughter and son-in-law explaining the patient's current hospital course and also the tenuous nature of the situation and the potential for deterioration over the subsequent days**. Also, given that the patient's CT angiogram had demonstrated an occlusion of the left carotid artery extending into the middle cerebral artery, I contacted Dr. George Teitelbaum of neuro-intervention in order to consider an interventional procedure should the patient's symptoms not improve; however, given the dramatic improvement in his neurological examination, we decided to hold off on any immediate intervention. The patient was admitted to the **critical care unit**.

SOCIAL HISTORY: He is an English professor.

FAMILY HISTORY: His son died of an aneurysm at age 20. Both of his parents died of myocardial infarctions.

REVIEW OF SYSTEMS: The patient currently is aphasic . . . however, he appears comfortable. He does not complain of any headache or chest pain . . .

GENERAL: He is alert. He has **expressive aphasia**. He is able to follow complex commands such as touching his left ear with his right thumb.

THE SECOND STROKE

The first half of the stroke had been bad enough, but the second half of the stroke – approximately seven days later – was more severe. Dr. (Roy) Antelyes sliced into the tissue at the base of the neck, but the massive stroke that I had had revealed the carotid artery, and it had turned stenotic. The internal carotid artery had been closed down into the occluding function to my brain, leaving the brain with three functions rather than four functions. Dr. Antelyes had no other choice to make. The brain function was collapsed on the left carotid side. From four to three inputs for language and other functions to flow toward the brain, to be processed, and to flow out from the brain! The second massive stroke separated the brain's incoming functions from the <u>coming together</u> of information and language to the <u>outgoing functions</u> that involved language communication in all of its forms.

However, when I awoke from the second stroke, Jo told me that the "left middle carotid artery stroke" had been totally "occluded." The brain had previously maintained a partially open door with blood flowing through to the brain and back again (my version), but the left carotid artery had been closed down permanently. The evidence was clear to the doctor: ". . . that the filling of the brain is permanently occluded. With the new finding of the carotid artery being occluded, the evidence is not to pursue the revascularization at this time with the greatly increased hazard . . . .". These functions included reading and listening, which worked as far as I could tell pretty well through the first and second stroke, to the other functions, **including writing and speaking, which had worked not at all since the second stroke**!

So I had no language whatsoever. One, two, three, four, five noises, and that was it. What did I feel like when I "recognized" the five noises but heard no language in any form? I was flat in bed, the right arm not working at all, and shorn clean of language. I felt totally blasted, totally wasted. The worst news of all that I could possibly imagine was to be without language. No language: I could not go any further down. I just couldn't imagine re-learning English again! I knew how much I had learned about it in the past -- the words, phrases, sentences, paragraphs, and chapters -- which equals the input, but I suddenly didn't know about <u>anything</u> about the whole business of speaking the language once again -- which equals the output!

Yet, I had to learn to speak again. I <u>knew</u> I had to learn, but I didn't even know what the English language was like any more: how it sounded, how it was shaped, and especially how it came across to people in a group. I didn't know a thing about how to respond to <u>any</u> of them. I had no idea about making a comment, asking a question, or even saying "I don't know!" or "What did you say?" I didn't know the first thing anymore about responding, expressing puzzlement, registering high praise, showing disgust, or joking. I had to build up these two purposes of language entirely from scratch.

In retrospect, I "saw" that in my case, reading and listening were the easier functions, and the harder ones were writing and speaking. The output was much more taxing – the writing and, particularly, the speaking – than the two input ones - the reading and the listening. Reading was the easiest. Somehow the reading wasn't really affected at all. Then came listening which was less easy. I was confused with the sound of some sentences as opposed to other sentences that I did hear quite clearly and remembered for some time. Writing was in third place, but it had become somewhat less difficult to manage than speaking. For me, speaking was the most difficult function of all the methods of communication. Speaking consistently lagged behind writing. But, when I finally imagined that the words could work for me and for those around me, I began to work at reuniting myself with the other people. But, I was dead slow and haltingly unfamiliar as I began the work of writing and speaking.

Before the stroke, I had a mastery of Italian. But now, I was missing Italian (a fact that it took me a little longer to see), because I was totally trapped in English. A little later, though, I did begin to know that the input was in Italian as well as in English. Actually, I was re-learning a little of the input side of English and Italian, though not everything about it was intelligible even after a bit of time had passed. But, a small piece of the language was Italian, and it was Italian that I found increasingly familiar and intelligible as far as the input was concerned. I had a bit more of the whole input side of the languages: English, which I could handle, and Italian, which I could also pretty much handle. But I wasn't able to handle English or Italian output at all. I began the long trek necessary to understand the output of two languages. So consequently, I was out of commission for two languages.

DATE OF OPERATION: 12/28/2009

POSTOPERATIVE DIAGNOSIS: Acute left hemispheric stroke, carotid artery disease and possible sub-clavian disease.

PROCEDURE(S) PERFORMED: Arteriogram of the aortic arch, intra-arterial injection of heparin, selective arteriogram of left carotid artery, cervical and left carotid artery, cranial.

INDICATIONS AND FINDINGS: . . . with acute left hemispheric stroke with aphasia and right hemiplegia. He was administered t-PA with substantial improvement. **His neurologic condition waxed and waned. Currently he is aphasic having at one point regained his ability to speak**. Imaging studies have been somewhat confusing in terms of their results. The left carotid artery to be occluded prior to t-PA, open subsequent to t-PA; however, carotid duplex scan this morning revealed the internal carotid artery to be occluded. On the first carotid scan the left sub-clavian artery may not be stenotic and thus, the indication for catheter angiography. At the time of the procedure, he was found to have normally configured aortic arch. The origins of the great vessels were patent and non-stenotic . . . The left sub-clavian artery gave rise to normal vertebral and internal mammary arteries . . . The left thoracic common carotid artery was normal. On subsequent imaging, the left carotid artery revealed extremely high-grade pre-occlusive stenosis in its proximal portion. The distal internal carotid artery was patent, but exhibited very slow flow . . .

The patient tolerated the procedure well. There were no complications. Blood loss was minimal. **The patient was transferred to critical care unit in stable condition**.

FINAL DIAGNOSIS:
1.   **Left internal carotid stenosis, pre-occlusive**

Robert P. Parker, PhD

DATE OF OPERATION: 12/30/2009

POSTOPERATIVE DIIAGNOSIS: Occluded internal carotid artery.

PROCEDURE(S) PERFORMED: Exploration of carotid artery and left carotid arteriogram.

INDICATIONS AND FINDINGS: The patient is a 72-year-old college professor who was admitted with a left hemispheric stroke. He was given systemic t-PA. His condition improved. Angiography on December 28 revealed very highly stenosis but still patient left internal carotid artery. The patient's neurologic condition had been unstable, thus, he had not had intervention prior to this time. Yesterday morning the patient had worsened neurologic symptoms. CT angiogram appeared to demonstrate a patent internal carotid artery, although it was poorly opacified.

PROCEDURES: With the patient in a supine position, he was prepared and draped in a sterile fashion . . . The common carotid artery was identified and isolated. It was encircled with a vessel loop and Rumel tourniquet. Access was gained to the distal internal carotid and it was controlled with a vessel loop. A 19-gauge butterfly needle was introduced into the common carotid artery and carotid arteriogram was performed. There was no evidence seen at all of filling of the internal carotid.

The patient tolerated the procedure well. There were no complications. He was transferred to the recovery room in stable condition.

With the new finding of the carotid artery being occluded, it was determined not to pursue revascularization at this time because of the greatly increased hazard . . .

The patient tolerated the procedure well. There were no complications. He was transferred to the recovery room in stable condition.

Here is what the National Stroke Association says about memory loss and aphasia.

Memory Loss

Memory loss after a stroke is common, but not the same for everyone. There are many memories can be affected by the stroke.

- Verbal memory: memory of names, stories and information having to do with words (National Stroke Association, 2014, n.d.). Names go in and out of focus all the time for me. One instant I have it all correctly remembered, but the next time it is a blank. Information and stories I remember better than names. There are problems with this one too, but not as severely as is the case for names.
- Visual memory: memory of faces, shapes, routes and things you see (National Stroke Association, 2014, n.d.)
- Therapies or medicines almost never fully restore memory after a stroke. But many people do recover at least some memory spontaneously after a stroke (National Stroke Association, 2014, n.d.). I recovered some memory spontaneously after the strokes.
- Others improve through rehabilitation (National Stroke Association, 2014, n.d.). Some do make improvement, and some don't improve at all. As for the ones who definitely make improvement, the tasks go slowly and are a long time coming. Maybe they are not quite making the improvement that had been expected, but they definitely get better in the long run.

What may help:

> Try to form a routine, doing certain tasks at regular times during the day.
> Try not to tackle too many things at once. Break tasks down into steps.
> If something needs to be done, make a note of it or do it right away.
> Make a habit of always putting things away in the same place where they can be easily seen or found (National Stroke Association, 2014, n.d.).

Aphasia

After a stroke, one of the most common thinking problems is trouble with communication. Aphasia is one of these problems. About one million people in the United States have aphasia. Most cases are the result of strokes (National Stroke Association, 2014, n.d.). Aphasia is a partial or total loss of the ability to read, to listen (or understand what people have to say), to write, and to talk. In my case, there was a "clear" divide between my input – the reading and the listening -- and my output – the writing and the speaking. I don't think reading was affected by the strokes, at least not as far as I can tell. I could read anything, including a nonfiction book called Complexity; The Emerging Science at the Edge of Order and Chaos by M. Mitchell Waldrop and a fiction book called The Winter's Vault by Anne Michaels. Each one is different from the other, so it is not the reading that is affected by the stroke, but the type of reading I am doing at the time.

The second factor, listening, was somewhat affected by the stroke, though more by the expressive aphasia than by the listening per se. It has to do with the stroke. I can only listen to one 'thing" now, the one that I am focused on right this second, not other similar things that before the stroke I could keep in separate or different parts of my mind, basically all at the same time. Now, post-stroke, I can't rely on the multiple things to remind me that I have two or three things in mind right now. The two or three things that I have now are gone to the aphasia-related stroke. I have lost the capacity to know the two things. I only know now the current thing, not the immediate past thing. I cannot remember two things at the same time. Permanently or temporarily, I don't know the answer to that yet.

Writing is the third most difficult task for me. But, it also gradually gets easier for me through practice, and the writing has become longer, more complex, and increasingly subtle. The speaking is the hardest one to do. Every day, I "practice" words that I will "express" to someone else. I practice before I speak them, silently and vocally, during the time when I am actually speaking them, and after I have spoken them. It does get gradually easier, however with great difficulty, but it does matter to me a lot. What matters is that the words are right to me silently, before I speak, and then after I have spoken. I think, though, that no matter how long it will be, it will be far into the future from what I can tell now.

It may affect only one aspect of language. For example, you may be unable to remember the names of objects or to put words into sentences. More often, many aspects are affected at the same time.

There are several types of aphasia. They differ according to which part of the brain is damaged: global aphasia; non-fluent aphasia; fluent aphasia; expressive aphasia. You may recover from aphasia without treatment. Most, however, benefit from therapy by a speech and language therapist. The goal is to improve your ability to communicate with other people. This is done by helping you get back some of your language skills and learning new ways of getting your message when needed.

- Use props to make conversation easier (photos, maps).
- Draw or write things on paper.
- Take your time. Make phone calls or try talking to people only when you have plenty of time.
- Show people what works best for you.
- Stay calm. Take one idea at a time.
- Create a communication book that includes words, pictures, and symbols that are useful to you.
- The Internet can be used to talk to people via e-mail or to create a personal web page for yourself (National stroke Association, 2014, n.d.).

*   *   *   *   *   *

THE PLASTIC FOOD TUBE

The doctors couldn't tell whether my throat would "accept" swallowing food or not. The doctors thought it might get better eventually, but they also said it might not. However, to protect the throat from further scarring, the doctors had ordered a plastic tube to be installed in my stomach, just below the fifth rib. The doctors told Jo that they had ordered the tube to be attached at both ends: straight up above to the hanging bag, into which the "mush" was inserted, and straight down to the stomach where the "mush" would dissolve.

Twice the doctors ordered it. The first time, they tried to put the plastic tube down the esophagus and then into the stomach. Once they read from the x-ray that the plastic tube was misaligned, they pulled it out and started again. So again, the doctors entered the plastic tube into the nose, put it down the esophagus, and then into the stomach, but the tube was still misaligned according to the second x-ray. Twice, they had ordered the x-ray to see what the doctors had accomplished, and twice the x-ray found that the doctors had misaligned the stomach tube.

So they decided to try a different kind of solid tube, an outside tube. The tube entered the stomach just below the mid-stomach, and, this time, the tube did enter the stomach and did work. The stomach would be filled with the "mush" coming down the tube and then assimilated by the stomach. The doctors wanted to know if I could swallow. With Amy helping out, I could swallow all of the "mush," but with considerable difficulty. Nonetheless, the plastic tube went on for about three weeks or more, and I "ate" three meals a day from the "mush."

Finally, I was taken off the feeding tube. It was about a week and a half before the end of my stay in the hospital, and I was given an ordinary hospital diet. Salmon, mashed potatoes, and string beans, or chicken, mashed potatoes, and carrots: one day the salmon, and the veggies and the next day the chicken and the veggies. The meals never varied. However, I had to truly take my time with the chicken or fish, the veggies, and the dessert. It took me about an hour or more to eat the food, and I had to stay very focused on the food right to the end of the meal.

The doctor who had installed the solid tube had originally done it well enough, but, unfortunately, the nurses didn't get the tube out nearly in time. The feeding tube remained in the "hole" where it entered just below the chest. It was in for six weeks: three before I left the hospital and three weeks after I left the hospital. So, Jo had to bring me back to the hospital, and the doctor took it out completely this time. What a tremendous relief. The solid tube was gone! It took a few days for the hole where the tube had been to close up. For a couple of weeks I had inspected the receding mark until I almost couldn't see it anymore.

Since the arm was totally "dead" on one side, every meal I had to eat was totally left sided and one-handed as well. Not until I gained the use of the right hand could I even start the process of extending my fork or spoon over to the right side. When I was discharged from the hospital, I made some small but steady gains in transferring my food to the right hand. I am still trying to shift the fork or spoon to the right hand, and every week I get better at using the hand the fork or the spoon with my right hand and not my left one. Now it has been three years since the stroke, and I'm still getting better at it.

THE "CIRCLE"

I can't remember when I was gathered "at the circle," but it was quite early in time. We were gathered around the nurse in charge, with everyone lying flat or sitting as up as they could. I was flat on my back, but Jo sat me up as high as possible in the wheelchair. Jo also said that it was "time" for the session to begin. "Time" is the proper word for it as I've learned now. The participants there with me were Jo, Jen, and Sandy. They all knew the word "time," and lots of other words too, but I couldn't even remember a single word.

Jo was there, as she was for everything that mattered to me! Jen and Sandy were "backing me up" too, although I didn't understand the point then. Actually, I hadn't made much sense of anything. I had to "interpret" it in a blur. I sort of did "get the meaning," but, also, I didn't get it! I would say "yes" to Jo or "no" to Jo, or to Jen or to Sandy, but without even the vague notion that I could possibly mean something to them. In effect, I couldn't speak to anyone! I could <u>hear</u> a bit of the sound coming in, but I could not <u>speak</u> externally at all!

Anyway, the nurse heading the department told us that we were "in the program." Also, the nurse explained that we all had to learn English <u>again</u>! The nurse said the statement because I sort of understood that phrase: "you have to learn English again" through input. This I could almost "get," though most of it was a blur. There were times when I could "understand" nearly everything, and times when I couldn't "understand" anything at all! It was because of expressive aphasia caused by the stroke.

I was 72, and I had to start learning English <u>again</u>. However, I didn't even know <u>how</u> to start learning the language again. Nor did I know <u>how</u> to continue to learn the language once I got it going. For some people of my age – or any age for that matter -- it is too hard for them edto begin again from scratch. They fail to begin at all, or, somewhere along the line, it gets too hard for them to continue to build up the English language. They tried and made certain gains, but they "failed" in the end.

I knew what that was like because that's where I was! I knew that I wanted to start with the language from the beginning, at the absolute, terrifying outset. This fact reflected a mind-boggling, stupefying but miraculous learning curve: literally one from the beginning of English to the "end," whatever that might turn out to be. Actually, there isn't an end: just a beginning and a middle. I don't know when anyone who knows what that end will be: certainly not me and not Jo. Maybe some doctors could be right about it, but I'm not even sure about that scenario. I was totally without words! I could attempt to make the noises into the sounds – yes, this is the real deal! -- the sounds into words, the words into phrases, and the phrases into sentences. At least I could possibly imagine doing it. But what a long struggle it was going to be for me, and for a lot longer into the future than I imagined it could ever have been at that point in time. Anyway, I was determined to start the language again**!**

During this time, though, I was flat on my back. I had no inkling that I could begin the long struggle to make the voice express the full range of the English language, to make the arm gain the ability to work, and to make the hand do what I wanted with it! Can you imagine these enormous, daunting tasks? The arm and the hand and the word and the voice: I couldn't even imagine being committed to each of one of those goals! The nurse told us that even before we left, with having to relearn the English language, beginning in the critical care unit – the critical care unit that I'd just been through -- and going on from there for the foreseeable future!

Can you think what that meant to <u>me</u> and to Jo, who understood that in response to her desperate desire to have me whole again? Now, I think I can in retrospect remember that voice inside of me and, later, outside of me. I remember now what it meant, but I'm not sure I could then have reasoned it out, let alone make sense of it. But now I know that the voice, arm, and hand could take much more time than I had thought to rebuild myself for the future!

And yet, when the nurse stood right in front of me, I couldn't hear a single word! I could hear only about five sounds, but not words! All of this was before anyone has spoken a "language" that I could understand. I could hear a bit of it, the input, but I couldn't speak any of it, the output. Understand the resonance of that issue for me, for Jo, and for the world: I had to re-learn English again! My attempt to speak came out as noises and sounds, but not, initially, as real words and phrases. In fact, I don't remember when the first words came out. Maybe it was when the therapist, Amy, took the first step toward me re-learning the entire language from scratch. I knew, though, that this word, the first word I had spoken, must have been badly formed and/or oddly shaped. But they must have come out eventually and idiosyncratically, in the stilted, garbled "English."

In fact, I had just begun to understand the difference between the input – the coming in –- and the output – the going out. I could now understand the "difference" between them, though only vaguely at this point. I could hear but not fully understand the words for the input, but I couldn't pronounce any of the words arranged in order as the output. I could sequence the order in one short thought, but I couldn't speak it in the next sentence. The nurse said this also because all the people who were there had strokes, although there were different types of them: ischemic stroke; embolic stroke; thrombosis stroke; large and small vessel stroke; and hemorrhagic stroke. But, the nurse who said this meant what she said! She knew what lay ahead for me and for all of her other patients as well.

Today, I have gotten clearer that at the time I knew the "I" noun and the "you" noun, and, subsequently, I came to know the verbs "could" and "could not." Now, I can "remember" four verbs: "could" or "could not" and "would" or "would not " in English, but painfully slowly at memorizing the four verbs! So, now, I could begin, "I could (not) . . . ", but I didn't know what the word would be for the next "blank," and it was a blank! It was absolutely like hitting a wall! Also, beyond that, strangely enough, or maybe not strangely at all, I couldn't remember the words at all from just a moment before when I had spoken them to Jo or to another person. Or, maybe I could remember them only fleetingly, and then they were gone in an instant. I had really forgotten them even though I had only "spoken" about them about two or three minutes ago!

I could remember the past words only vaguely. In fact, I couldn't recall what the sounds or words were after I had just uttered them! I couldn't recall even the very brief word, or words, or even phrases that came out of my mouth, just as though they had been "spoken" by someone else. What did "they" sound like to "me"? What did the "phrases" mean, if they meant anything at all? Who did I speak to in the previous minutes? What were "they" like to those persons who were the least bit familiar with these clues? Was it a "question" that I was asking? Was it a "comment" that I was trying to make? Was it an "observations"? Or a "jokes": although it was later on when that began to happen.

I find this amazing to look back in retrospect at the answer to this "question" or this "comment," but it was absolutely true for me. Perhaps, that fact is true for all stroke victims. I had to really proceed slowly about speaking the language for which I had just begun to learn the words again! It was difficult for me to remember all the words that I had spoken throughout the hour, let alone throughout the day. In fact, I had forgotten many of the words that I had just spoken. I am getting more certain now that I still have trouble remembering nouns, verbs, adjectives, adverbs, and pronouns, plus names and towns. I remember one minute and forget the next minute. I think that fact will be true all of my life! I will get better with the whole range of words, but not to the extent of remembering everything anymore! And the question is . . . but I don't know how to answer that question – yet! Although over time, I can understand the whole sentence and with increasing clarity and precision.

MY RIGHT ARM WAS "DEAD"

My right arm was literally dead. I think I could feel a bit further up the arm, but perhaps I couldn't feel anything at all. I could, though, put the arm into a sling, limply at first, which I did. I put the arm into a sling, and I took the arm out of the sling. In and out it came. Though the sling was quite useful toward the beginning of the journey, it gradually became just a sling. Now, over time, it has become increasingly useless to me, so I have jettisoned the sling entirely.

Over time, I have made some substantial progress in beginning to work on the arm, on the hand, and on the fingers. Take the arm first as an example: I could move the arm up just slightly and, then, bring it back to where it was originally. But next time, I could move it to where it is just a little bit up, not as it was then. Not much, but it was higher. Stretching the arm, again and again, I was able to force the arm to stretch up even higher still than it was originally. So the arm is higher up than it was before. All I still have to do is to lift the right arm up as far I am able to and stretch it out until it lifts as high as the other left arm.

The arm can now be stretched up as high as it can go. The arm can also be stretched out all the way as far as it can go, be stretched downwards as far as it can go, and be stretched backward as far as it can go. I worked to move it around, back and forth and up and down, and I found that it was real work to be able to move it in all four directions. But basically, I had to work the arm to bring it back to "life," literally. I had to do this many times for the right arm strength so that it could equally be as strong as the left arm. I did this over and over for almost four years. Eventually, the arms will move straight up and down. The arm is not totally back to normal, but it is getting much closer now. That's the goal of this part of the arm challenge.

Now I'm facing the elbow, wrist, and finger challenge. I've made some progress. The elbow feels even straighter than before. The right wrist is improving, too. It can bend back, bend forward, and bend sideways. So, the wrist is improving, but not the fingers yet. And it's not the correct way yet to stretch the wrist and hand out, but it's more adequate than my previous attempt to correct the strength and the flexibility of the wrist. Also, the right hand isn't as straight yet as the left hand is yet. Although the hand slowly makes strides as well. It's very subtle though, and it takes a long time for the right arm, the wrist, and the hand to work as well as the left hand works.

For four of the five fingers, I have worked to return them to normal again by stretching them in and out, by manipulating the fingers, and by stretching the fingers: two each, the thumb and forefinger and the fourth finger and fifth finger. First, I have been separating the thumb and forefinger over a year and half now a, trying to get the two fingers totally straightened out. The two fingers are straightening out, but not far enough yet. The two fingers force the thumb in, and the forefinger comes down over the top of the thumb. The thumb and forefinger have, though, relaxed the process a bit, and, by separating themselves, are trying to become even more flexible, getting closer together and coming apart.

Second, the two last fingers on the other side, the ring-finger and the little finger, are different from the thumb and forefinger. These two fingers are slowly making progress, but it is still stiff. The little finger has numbness all the way to the tip of the finger. The fourth finger has tightness on top and in the middle. So the last two fingers on the right side have some issues, but, nonetheless, they are doing as well as can be expected. And I just recently I have worked with the third finger as well, trying to make this finger work as well as the other four fingers.

In fact, the whole hand, which is still sore, but coming along, is also making progress toward the place where the right hand will be as completely functional as possible. I'll have to keep on working these fingers, because I don't know whether the right hand will work as well as the left hand does. But I know that it could take a while longer than I had anticipated.

STEVE

My brother, Steve Parker, came from Butte, Montana, to Pasadena two times. I remember him taking care of me in the intensive care unit of the hospital. Jo went home for two or three hours to make a call, to take a shower, put on some different clothes, or take a nap. During those times, I remember Steve visiting with me alone. When I awakened, he would put away his computer or stop reading his newspaper.

Mainly, Steve spoke as slowly as he could, and I listened as well as I could. He also watched me when I talked to him, and tried to understand what I wanted to get across to him. I have vivid memories of while he waited patiently for me to finally realize the one thing that I did want to give to him, get from him, or, even better, go and tell Jo. The one thing that I could get across to him, and what I wanted to articulate to him, however feebly that might be, would be the smallest part of the whole text I had "imagined" speaking. Although, most of the time, I just could not get it "through" to anyone: not to Steve, or Jo or to anyone else.

Some of the time I was awake for a few minutes or perhaps an hour, but then I would drift off to sleep again. But Steve was persistent and patient. Sometimes, while I was awake, he talked with me, or I should say he talked at me. I was aware of him, but I just couldn't answer back. My mouth and tongue would not do it. No matter what he said, I would say, "I can . . ." or "I could . . ." and that's all. I could begin the statement but not end the statement. However, just by my drawing a blank at that point in time, it didn't matter to him that I could not finish the statement. He would take as much time as he had available, and he would take it to Jo and make it as clear as he could. He tried hard, and he finally got what I wanted him to say, or at least part of what I was attempting to say to him and pass it along to Jo or to another person.

THE "SCRUNCH" AND THE WHEELCHAIR

I was flat in bed for most of the first week after the second stroke. The nurses took a twenty-four hour shift. Round the clock, Jo and the nurses took care of me. After a week or so, the nurses scrunched me up on one side and made the bed on the far side, and then the nurses turned me over to the other side and completed making the bed on the near side. The nurses also took my temperature morning, noon, and night, changed my clothes, gave me a bath -– both in bed and in the bathroom, checked the bed sore on my back, set me up for watching TV whether low or mid-range or high, changed my clothes, tied my shoes, and so on. The nurse also had a breathing device that I could blow into and out again, and I slowly got better at that, too.

At that point, a nurse brought the wheelchair in for me to see if I could make it into the chair or not. This was a brand new experience: from the bed, standing up, and into the wheelchair. But I sat there before I moved at all in the direction of the wheelchair, let alone attempted to climb into it. Shortly, the nurse instructed me how to move into the wheelchair, which I did with great difficulty, and then took me for a short walk. That is the first time I have been into the hallway, other than rolling into the hospital room flat on my back. Then, the nurses, and eventually Jo, came to take me for longer and longer walks: walking around inside the building, over to the café or the snack bar, and sometimes outside the building as well.

For a time, it was sufficient for me to travel here and there in the wheelchair pushed by the nurse or Jo. But, when I stood erect, even for a moment and out of the wheelchair, I asked the staff for a brief period to be allowed to move freely for a second or two and for me to walk without holding on to anything else except for the wall and the cane. So, on my feet, I held onto the wall and the cane for a brief moment and then sat back down again in the wheelchair. But, a few days later, I was standing alone with nothing but the cane. So I asked the staff if it would be all right to move just a little alone with the cane. To my surprise, all alone, no hands on anything else including the wall, holding on to nothing except the cane, I moved just a bit. But I did move, and it had worked! Slowly, over the days, I then walked a little further along the wall and then sat down again in my wheelchair, which the nurse had brought along with me.

The nurses had to make my exercise time even longer. I can remember that entire phase: to remain seated in the wheelchair; to stand up from the wheelchair; to walk with the wall and the cane as far from the wheelchair as possible and back to the wheelchair; and to walk slowly with cane only and back to the wheelchair! It took me a week or so to walk even that far, but I did do it. I actually walked the whole distance – slowly, but I did it! I walked down the hallway, around the corner, and back again. The next day, in order to walk even a greater distance, I attempted to make this entire walk around the corner once, and then I had to walk back around the corner again. At first, this was once, but then it got increased to twice! Finally, I did it four times! I had to walk <u>four</u> times around the hallway and <u>four</u> times back. I did it, four times, but I was really tired when it ended! But I was psyched, too.

ADMIT DATE: 02/02/10:
*

HOSPITAL COURSE: . . . He was admitted to the rehabilitation ward to address the functional deficits.

While in the rehabilitation ward, he received intensive services with physical therapy, occupational therapy, speech and dysphasia services. He made reasonably good progress. **He was able to raise the right upper extremity against gravity, but hand function was impaired.** In the right lower extremity, he had reasonably good synergy.

His swallowing improved. He received dysphasia services.

At discharge from the rehabilitation ward, he required supervision for bed transfers and chair transfers, car transfers supervised, gait 250 feet times 3 transferred. He required set up for grooming, minimal assistance for bathing, upper body dressing modified independent, lower body dressing minimal assistance, toileting modified independent, toilet transfer modified independent. From a language standpoint, he was oriented times 4: problem-solving moderated impairment (and) moderated impairment for memory skills. **Auditory comprehension required moderated prompting for simple information, yet he was inconsistent. Verbal expression, he required total assistance.**

ACTIVITY: He will have outpatient physical therapy, occupational therapy, and speech therapy services.

JO

Jo did everything for me, totally! She immediately took over the expenses and the bills. She watched while I had my hospital breakfast, lunch, and dinner. I didn't know how to wipe myself, and she taught me how to do it. She washed me all over. She lathered me up first, but she watched me while I washed the soap off. Then she took the shampoo and helped me put it on and take it off. But she took the conditioner in order for me to put it on by myself.

In addition, she talked with the nurses all the time. I didn't have the will or the language to do this with the nurses. Jo cared a lot about all the medications, as well she might have. She asked, "What are you doing with this medication?" Or she asked, "Why are you giving him this medication?" She asked a special nurse, "Why are you giving him this pill? It's a stool softener!" And the nurse said, "Oh, yeah, I see now. I didn't read the medication. Sorry." At another time, a nurse was giving me my medication whole when it had to be crushed. Jo was able to cut down on my medications quite a bit over time. In the face of chaos, she created a way to get it done. It was the two of us versus the world at large!

She watched while I took a short walk with a nurse helping me along, a short walk without help, a longer walk with close but no assistance, then a slightly longer one more or less by myself, and then long walk with no assistance. She did take short breaks when she went out for a while, but only when I had a meal brought into the room with a nurse supervising, or she had Jen and/or Sandy in the room.

When I arrived at home, Jo's work shifted, and she took over when I had my meals at home. She still had to do all the preparations: fixing all the fish, chicken, tofu, salad, vegetables, desserts, and so on. Slowly though, I learned how to do all the rest, including clearing the table and cleaning up afterwards. First, though, she had to do all the washing up. But now she does only some of it, and I do the rest. By the way, I don't like to do the pots any more now than I did in the past, but I do the bowls, the dishes, and the silverware. And I am still doing more today than I used to do.

At first, she had to wash all of my clothes. Over the months, however, I gradually learned how to do it. Now, she does none of my clothes anymore. I also now strip the bed, wash the sheets and pillowcases, and re-make the bed. And I do it with the hand that gets better but isn't quite ready yet.

MARK

Jo saw that I was safely with Mark, a friend. She could then leave a myriad of other things to do outside the hospital. She could leave me with Mark, whether I was just sitting on top of the bed or in the wheelchair ready to go. Mark, however, did for me something that I will always love him for: talked, listened, massaged me, let me fall back to sleep again, or walked me out to the garden. Three or four times he came to the hospital room to talk with me, although he was mostly the one who spoke. Most importantly, though, he could listen, could answer me back, or even more, just not talk at all.

He came to take me for a walk to wherever I wished to go. He saw to it that I had a wheelchair and put me into it for the ride outside to the garden. Sometimes, I just relaxed. Anyway I couldn't talk much, and he stayed silent, too. But at other times I had questions for him. I tried hard to make the questions understandable to him, but it wasn't easy! Much of the time, when I talked with Mark, at least as far as my communication with him was concerned, I got my questions sort of answered. I mean, he answered them, but I'm not sure that I understood all the responses. Mark answered them all, or least he tried to. I know that some of the answers I received were "real" as he said them to me, but not every one made sense to me at least at that point in time. His responses were right on, but mine were, well, somewhat on the mark and somewhat off the mark. Actually, he didn't seem to mind whether I would get this feedback or not; he would say it again and, if necessary, once again. He would just sit there while I reveled in the sun. Nonetheless, these afternoon talks or rests were a special kind of peacefulness, especially out there in the garden when it became nicer and more pleasant.

Mark started a routine while in the hospital room, and he finished it in the condo. He would massage my fingers, my hand, and my arm. He started with the fingers, moved to the arm, and finished with the shoulder. The hand started to tingle; then the elbow started to tingle, too; and then the arm started to tingle as well. Mark not only exercised the fingers, the hand, and the shoulder, but it felt better every time I had this treatment. The massage Mark gave me lasted about three to four hours.

But other times he just talked, and at other times he just listened to me. I didn't realize it then, but I know now how those thoughts might end up carrying me on, and into, the expanding conversation I wanted so desperately to have. All the other people had things to say to people who would listen. They were things that I wanted to hear myself, and they were things that I might have wanted to say to someone else. But I just couldn't do it at that time. Though now, I have increased quite remarkably in the length and duration of the conversations I am having -- and plan to continue to have – with Jo, with Mark, at the Jones Coffee House, and, eventually, at the Sambalatte Café much later on. But, for the time being, Jo and Mark were more responsible for that fact than anyone.

For example, at the condo, I would spend an hour or two in the afternoon with Mark, mainly out and about in the neighborhood! We would head up the road ready to go wherever I wanted to go and whenever I wanted to come back. I could go with the wheelchair, standing up but with the cane, without the cane but handheld for safety, or totally without the cane. Over this period of time I had first taken the wheelchair outside and was pushed along by Mark. Then, I left the wheelchair behind, and, in fact, the staff picked it up for good. So, I stood up and walked, slowly, but I walked. One time I even walked to the art museum and back again! I used the cane for walking, but, after a while, I had taken the cane but used it infrequently. Then I stopped taking the cane altogether.

It seems like a small measure, and in a way it was for Mark, but for me it was a big deal. I was truly free to go wherever I wanted! I had discovered a new determination and a new way to independence! Mark was amazing in pursuit of this goal. He was totally focused on getting me out there in the world. He was also graceful, honest, committed to the task at hand, and entirely self-effacing.

JEN AND SANDY

All forty-three days I was in the hospital, then one night out, and back in for another five nights. Jen or Sandy, sometimes both of them, hung out with me, but also they helped me when I was in the intensive care unit and the rehabilitation unit where I was getting prepped for the final route to my home. Jo hadn't slept in the condo either for forty-three days, so Jen and/or Sandy filled the bill for me. I can remember both of them lounging about, bringing food and magazines, and bringing me clothes. Jen and/ or Sandy was there, and sometimes they stayed with me until I got ready for bed. Sometimes one, or both, of them stayed while Jo took a breather from me to go the condo in order to take a shower, to put on some clean clothes, and to pay some bills. But, Jo didn't stay away from me for more than two or three hours at a time. In fact, she would come back with a new bag repacked for the trip back to the hospital. When the late afternoon or the night came, Jo was back again for yet another evening and night: for the forty-three evenings she spent with me.

AMY

Amy, my speech therapist, had fourteen or fifteen sessions with me in the hospital room. Right from the start, without Amy I couldn't have done any of it, either inside the hospital or outside the hospital. When she started with me, I had no language at all! I could "see" the picture of the rabbit or squirrel or snake (or whatever it was), but I had no word for "it." So she taught me the first word I pronounced – the sound "I." Then she taught me the word for the second session: "I could," and the word for the third session: "I could not."

After I had been discharged from the hospital, we then set up a series of sessions that lasted about six months. Since then, I have learned, painfully and stressfully, to articulate the learning process ever more clearly. Over and over again I tried to pronounce the words, with the right hand sitting in a sling on top of the table not moving, the left hand spelling the sounds out, and then speaking out the sounds with some kind of voice mechanism. What a horrible, excruciating process that was – and is now! For example, "I could . . ." say that much, but that's all I could say! I could remember the words at the beginning of the sentence, but a blank always occurred at the end of the sentence. How to say them in sequence, from beginning to end, what an incredible process that was. It was a painstaking process, but I continued to make even longer strings of words over time. Some days I even finished a sentence! A shortish one, mind you, but I was extremely glad to have that sentence finished. Some days I moved rapidly ahead, and some days I reverted. Sometimes I really didn't know what was what.

Amy and I met in my room (eventually, when I was out of the hospital, it became Amy's room), and I tried and tried and tried some more – with Amy's insistence and support, but primarily her intention as to what she wanted me to get out from "inside" – inside my brain -- to "outside" –- to the world! She <u>intended</u> me to pronounce more and more words correctly! I produced some very painful phrases, some "kind of like" sentences, although there were some good sentences, too. Whenever I got from the beginning to the end of the sentence, it was a single sentence! But, when I got there, whatever I had just learned through imitation or through sense-making, I realized that I had much, much more to learn as well: more to pronounce, certainly, but, even more, to use language as much as possible with the widest range of application available. That was Amy's goal.

Amy slowly, gradually, taught me to pronounce the words more clearly, more precisely, and more articulately. More and more words were coming together; more and more phrases were coming together; and more and more sentences were coming together! But I had to speak the words slowly, carefully, and clearly from start to finish. I started one sentence after another as clearly as I could at that point, yet I still blanked at making sure that the sentences started the way that they finished. I could start the word or words to begin the sentence, but I couldn't finish it. Even now, I still <u>think</u> I can finish it, but there still remains "blanks" of words where the right word seems absent. Or, I can almost hear it -- it's in my mind though not in my voice – but I can't quite spit it out. In my mind, it's clear, but in my speech, it isn't quite clear! Gradually, though, there is an increasing "bank" of words, phrases, and sentences that makes my speech clearer, longer, and more complex. I really am getting better at what I have to say to people: what the <u>intent</u> is, and what the <u>meaning</u> is.

I am also getting better at figuring out what word or words go into sentences and what words come out of sentences: calculating what phrases and sentences they are, and are not, and figuring out about tracking and adjusting for their usefulness to my intended meaning. I am more right than wrong about the remembered word, also the words and the sentences. I am still tracking down the right word, or words, but less now than I was initially. In fact, I am doing much less tracking down the memories, particularly my more recent memories. There seems to be more of a "blend" between what I am trying to say and what I just said. Although, I am continuing to chase down the "blanks" right up to the present moment and beyond, but I'm down to two or three now. I am getting much better in my choice of words, phrases, and sentences, particularly the combination of choices among sentences. I had to make sure that the words that we worked on were the ones that I needed from the beginning to the end: mix and match, match and mix. I still fought with my mind and my voice, and it still goes on! It will probably never stop, not with the aphasia.

I recognized that aphasia had a lot of bearing on what I <u>did</u>, but it had so much more than that to do with the range of things that I had <u>to learn</u> about. I had begun to think gradually about my disposition toward the whole facet of language, especially nouns, verbs, adverbs, and adjectives! I had "forgotten" what I knew for fifty years: the grammar! It was the nouns and the verbs that woke me up. I had known that for a long time, but the stroke "took" that memory away. These are the troublesome ones, nouns and verbs; they are the biggest part of the challenge, but also the biggest part of the solution. But Amy knew all of that and more too!

I don't remember each exercise that I did in the beginning, perhaps because they weren't ones that I could recognize. Amy paced the lesson out so that I could catch on a little bit at a time, but it wasn't very much at all. Gradually though, around April 2010, I began working on a series of individual words which did make more sense: then sentences, then paragraphs, and finally short stories that also made even more sense! I also had a "word dis-order," one in which the words were rearranged or backwards. I had to sort them out so they made sense together rather than separately, and those particular ones came either in three sentences or four sentences or five sentences. Slowly, I get better at arranging the words so that they made sense.

I've come a really long way from the beginning, when I didn't have a word to say audibly. Now with a solid, painstakingly assembled, background of nouns, verbs, adjectives, and adverbs I can say it out loud more accurately than in the past few months. Sometimes I would get a sentence started but still was unable to finish it, or, if I did, it seemed like a great sentence until the very end. Many times I started a sentence with a real intension of finishing it, but I ended up getting stuck, experiencing the word that I "needed" but couldn't find it anywhere in my vocabulary, and then I abandoned the search altogether. At the other end of it though, I could complete a few sentences that initially I had abandoned.

Now, at this point, I am able to make words not only into a sentence but also into at least two or three sentences. Actually, I could start a conversation, and I could participate in it for a little while, but, by the same token, I could not finish it off. At least I could start speaking and get a good way through the sentence. But, a brief time later, I could develop a conversation, and then, with no more than two people, I potentially could finish it as well! Amy had a great deal to do with my early learning of English. Today it continues on apace as the Jones Coffee Roasters, Sambalatte, and Café Leone. I like the Samba Quantum Tribe, and I will speak with them more clearly, more precisely, and for longer periods of time. It first was Amy, and then, increasingly, once I was on my own, and it was Jo and a host of other friends.

PART III
FINDING THE NEW ME

"Of course a stroke isn't identical to aging; I didn't get any older because I had a stroke. But it is a new chapter in my aging process. The final stage of aging is cuddling up to death, and the stroke gave me some experience with that."

Ram Dass, <u>Still Here: Embracing Aging, Changing, and Dying</u>

*   *   *   *   *   *   *   *   *

A BRIEF – IN FACT, ONE NIGHT – WELCOME HOME

I was in the long-term care part of the hospital facility. I had been taken to the west wing, to the fourth floor, and to the transition from the hospital back to our condo. It was a nice room, quite large, and on the end where we could see the sky through the two sets of windows. When I went there to stay for three weeks, it was to prime me for the end of my visit to the hospital. But, I was outside the hospital for one day, and then I was back inside the hospital for five more days.

First though, Jo and I had a very warm welcome home. Jen, Sandy, and Michaela, a close friend, were there, and, when I walked in, I received great hugs, long kisses, and gala banners. "Welcome home, Bob." it said across the front window. I hugged and kissed Jo, and then I hugged the rest of them. It was quite a party for Jo, Jen, Sandy, and Michaela, but it was a very special party for me and for Jo. We were at home at long last! I couldn't speak much then, but I had a great party nonetheless.

However, I was released only for a single day, and now I was back in the hospital again. I had been very excited about getting home, and I had a good night's sleep. But, after only one day out of the hospital, I found myself falling downward to the bathroom floor, though slowly, but I still hadn't lost consciousness. Jo exclaimed, "Help me up!" and I thought quietly as I slid down until I could slump on the floor slowly on top of Jo! But she was underneath me, and I heard her say, "What do I do now?" Fortunately, she had her cell phone in hand. So Jo called the 911 numbers, and the paramedics came quickly. After they had arrived and checked me out, asking me a few questions, they put me on a stretcher. I was taken back to the hospital and put into the emergency room to see if something again had happened.

The doctors seemed to agree that embolisms had traveled upward to my lungs. Actually, it was from both legs, but how long ago they were not sure! I was extremely tired, discouraged, and depressed beyond belief, but Jo was the one who really heard it all. Only vaguely did I know what emboli were, but Jo knew more than I knew. The doctors thought it was likely it had been embolisms, but the doctors and Jo agreed that there was no way that we could know exactly what had happened.

It just doesn't seem fair to be spending forty-three days in the hospital, and then to be out for one day and back in the hospital again after only one night at home. Now, I was back in the hospital for another five days! The nurses placed me back in bed and lying flat again. Lying down and sitting up was all I could do, rather than standing up or walking around with the cane. However, after the first three days, I was able to stand up, but only to walk two or three steps out to the chair and two or three steps back until I was in bed again. The chair was right next to the bed, but that's all I could do.

But I finally gained strength, and, from the third day, I was able to stand up, walk down the hall, although not too far a distance, and walk back, but infinitesimally more slowly than I had walked before. And then, I can recall walking with the cane only just around the corner and then back again. Shortly after, I was back in bed again. After the doctors had checked me out thoroughly, they said that I did have embolisms in both legs, but they felt they were the "old" ones that I had had before. So I just would have to wait and see what showed up next.

ADMIT DATE: 02/03/2010

HISTORY OF PRESENT ILLNESS: This 72-year old male is status post-stroke about eight weeks ago with residual right facial droop and right-sided paresis, but no expressive or receptive aphasia. He has been home for a few days. **He got up and was walking and had a near-syncopal episode. He collapsed and was caught by his family, so there was no injury.**

GENERAL: Well-nourished, well-developed male in no acute distress, alert and oriented, pleasant and cooperative.

NEUROLOGIC: Strength on the right side 4 to 4+/5, right upper extremity and right lower extremity, and 5/5 on the left.

DIAGNOSIS: Acute pulmonary emboli.

ADMIT DATE: 02/03/10

HISTORY OF PRESENT ILLNESS: . . . He now presented with near syncope. He denied having dizziness but while he was in the bathroom he collapsed and had weakness. His wife tried to help him but both slowly went to the floor. He denied any chest pain, no palpitation, no nausea, no vomiting, no diaphoresis. **He did have shortness of breath . . .**

Robert P. Parker, PhD

ADMIT DATE: 02/03/10

REASON FOR CONSULTATON: Initiation of anticoagulation for pulmonary embolism.

HISTORY OF PRESENT ILLNESS: The patient is . . . very well-known to me from a recent hospitalization between the dates of December 22, 2009 through his inpatient stay of January 8, 2010. The patient had initially with a left middle cerebral artery stroke and was found to have a severe left internal carotid artery stenosis. A carotid endarterectomy had been planned . . . Unfortunately, at the time of his planned surgery, it had been noted that his carotid was occluded and therefore no intervention was done. The patient was left with a residual right hemi-paresis as well as expressive aphasia. He did very well from a rehabilitative standpoint (and) was able to regain some approximately in his right upper extremity. He was ambulating normally. He was also able to have some speech output which was significantly improved from the time of his presentation.
. . . when he suddenly felt weak and short of breath, and collapsed to the floor . . . His wife had contacted EMS . . . Since being in the emergency room, he has undergone a CT angiogram of his chest which has demonstrated extensive pulmonary emboli throughout the right middle and lower lobes . . . I have been consulted to help with decision making regarding anti-coagulation given his recent stroke. He is otherwise without complaints.

NEUROLOGICAL/MENTAL STATUS EXAMINATION: **. . . he has minimal speech output. He has a non-fluent aphasia. He follows the majority of commands correctly. He has mild difficulty with complex commands. Fund of knowledge is reduced.**

SUMMARY: . . . The patient is brought in for a new pulmonary embolism. His neurological examination is unchanged from the time of discharge. I do not suspect that he has had a new neurologic event.

I would, however, obtain a non-contrast head CT to rule the possibility of hemorrhagic transformation of his stoke prior to initiated anticoagulation which he will require for his pulmonary embolism. I would also recommend obtaining hyper-coagulable testing as it is quite unusual for someone to have with both a stroke as well as a pulmonary embolism in such a short time period for someone with no medical history . . .

ADMIT DATE: 02/23/10

HISTORY OF PRESENT ILLNESS: . . . with history of a left middle cerebral artery stroke on December 22, 2009. He had a right-sided paralysis and aphasia for which he went to rehabilitation on January 8, 2010 and did really well.

. . . for pulmonary embolism and, as a result, was paced on Coumadin . . . According to his wife, he was doing really well. **His speech was recovering. He was moving his right arm more, and he was doing well with rehabilitation.** However, this morning he got up feeling that the right side of his body was numb and weak, and he could not get up, stand up or walk.

Paramedics were called . . . He does feel back to his normal self, although he feels some changes on the right side especially with his vision and sensation. He is not quite able to communicate.

MENTAL STATUS: He is awake and alert, oriented to place and time. He answers questions appropriately. **He does have trouble with fluency and with expressive aphasia.**

DISCUSSION: His neurological examination is not much different from when last he was seen in the hospital, and, in fact, he may have made improvement with his speech. He presents with these changes that he cannot quite explain on the right side face and body. Some of them may be visual changes. It is not clear if this is an exacerbation of his old symptoms or a new stroke. He certainly is at risk for new cerebro-vascular accident.

Robert P. Parker, PhD

THE REAL EXTENT OF LANGUAGE

I know what the intention and the meaning are of the English language in input. However, I nearly cried because of the total amount of words that had to be learned versus output. I didn't even know what the words were! When we started to talk, however haltingly, I could partly understand the full extent of what I was totally lacking in discourse! I could not explain the almost total lack of language I had at this point to Jo or to anyone else, although the other people around me seemed to get part of it. They knew I could not speak, and they knew that it would take me a long time. Nonetheless, I determined that if speaking could be re-learned, why then I would learn to speak again – completely and faster than it usually takes.

Over more than three years, I worked hard. Suddenly, so much faster than I could have foreseen, things clicked. I was really happy when these things started to happen. At the same time, I was also terribly depressed. Nothing seemed to be working. Things work hand in hand: sometimes a total moment of elation and sometimes a moment of total depression. At the time, I sobbed asking Jo for support and comfort. Both of these events happened! I worked hard and nothing came! Yet, on the other hand, suddenly something came clear for me. Two things that didn't make sense to me at all. Now I know that they do make sense, with the memory inching forward and the aphasia pushing me backward, though I don't know how to explain that to anyone else. I'm not even sure that I understand it totally. But when the concept makes sense to me, at least partially, it might possibly be making sense to you, too: if I can put it together very carefully, very clearly, very well expressed, and slowly enough for you to understand.

I simply could not get the words to come out! I was unhappy about that event and started to cry. I didn't cry very often, but I felt the "whoosh" go straight out of me. I felt paralyzed and hopeless because I thought that this was the whole piece of the language that I was attempting to express. I was down in the dumps about the whole act of speaking. Jo had to move into my space temporarily and calm me down before I could move forward again, to continue on my way toward an even greater degree of hopefulness. Now, I've had this whole speaking thing before, and I'll have it again:

infrequently, but enough to feel totally hopeless for a few minutes. Yet then, a few minutes later, I feel totally committed to carrying on as before. It is strange, but the notion of hopeless vs. commitment is commonly held. So I just carry on when I can and if I can: word by word, sentence by sentence, and paragraph by paragraph.

Slowly, and I mean slowly, I carried on learning a piece at a time, the parts that fold together into a conversation and with some degree of increasing focus and with some degree of precision. By then, I had moved on to a whole statement governed by whatever went on in the previous conversation and in the subsequent one. The whole statement had to be slowed down considerably, but not ended any more. When I spoke, I make longer and longer statements. I did so eagerly and intently, but they had to be much slower than I had experienced before. I also spoke sentences of greater length and of greater complexity, and I also spoke them gradually but completely. So, once again, I reacquired the awareness of speaking even more slowly than I had to speak in the past but more carefully, more clearly, and more precisely!

So, the pressure is on to steadily move toward increasing my capacity to become a participant in a conversation. Five minutes, no matter how short or how long it is, is not really the main issue. It is more likely I can become a full participant in a conversation. Nothing out of the ordinary, but in a conversation that continues some time at least for the two or three participants in it! It's a slowly increasing glimpse right now than it ever was before I began. Slowly, I'm in the process of getting better at it all the time. I can see the progress over the past few months. And, I have more options with the English language and more options with my arm and hand as well. All three are coming along fine!

TRYING TO CROSS THE LINE

I have read many books throughout my life. Nonfiction, fiction, poetry, and drama, and I will continue to read them avidly. So, I have lots of language arriving inward, and still more to come, including listening and reading. Moreover, I can use the language I have gained now for writing uses, but not yet for speaking. They are in my "head," but I can't get enough of these words out to satisfy me. Also, it is a rapidly expanding list of words. The nouns, verbs, adjectives, adverbs, and pronouns can be used for any purpose that I want to pursue. They are "ready" for any kind of use, and they can be all "wired" into the system, completely now, though more slowly than I would like.

I read Colm Toibin recently. His novel, <u>Brooklyn</u>, is a remarkable piece of prose writing. It is consistently and structurally grammatical in its organization, and the story is brilliant as well. Also, I have read two novels of Anne Michaels: <u>Fugitive Pieces</u> and <u>The Winter Vault</u>, plus two books of her poetry. Just as Colm Toibin is structured grammatically all the way through his entire book, Anne Michaels goes to the other extreme and structures her sentences as lyrical and poetic in her two books: Toibin, the grammatical writing on the one side, and Michaels, the lyrical and poetic writing on the other side. I can now expand even further the intention, meaning, and poetic use that can be defined by an abstract line stretched out in two directions: one lyrical and poetic and the other substantive and grammatical. It is much more now in vivid definition as an abstract and in substantive practicality for use than I had ever thought possible.

In my particular case, the input is expanding, and it is after the stroke! I can read all the words in the books, on the Kindle, and on the screen. I can lay them side by side, and they make absolute sense to me as input. But the output, the speaking, is still much smaller than the input. I can't "cross the line" between the input and the output! I can't cross the "step" between the two parts, though I am trying as hard as I can to make the "crossing" more possible. As I said, the input is solid enough, but the output is still troubled, still mixed up, though it is increasing as fast as I can go by adding more words, phrases, and sentences to the mix of words and sentences that I can use right now. However, will my head filling up with words that I can speak, right now or shortly, be enough? Or will that smear of words never be enough to try all the phrases and sentences? Will I still be frustrated?

The meaning of some of the sentences I am speaking – or we are speaking -- would be mostly clear to me and, perhaps, to you. Yet, some of the other sentences that I speak will be garbled so that the meaning and the intention are still at issue. I guess that is the case at least for right now: one complete and one garbled. I can speak what I want to say clearly enough to make it recognized, yet the <u>next sentence</u> may be off by a little bit or by a lot.

So the one sentence - or two or three – is clear and comprehensive, yet the next one is garbled. Or, if not exactly garbled, still not completely fluent and not quite complete when the grammar is "factored" in. Even though the fluency of the content and the grammar are getting better, there is still something wrong with it. I know what I am trying to say, but do you know what I mean? It sounds <u>virtually</u> fine to me, but how do I know what it sounds like to you? Also, I don't always know yet what the other person is saying to me. Is it clear on both sides of the presentation? Sometimes it is like a puzzle to me, but sometimes it is not. All the words are quite clear. And it is <u>my</u> problem, not yours. Your meaning is clear, but it is mine. That is the issue.

Two strokes make the difference. I have the aphasia "built in," and I don't know how or why that is the issue. But it is. I have a few words to put out right now, though that will increase over time. In fact, the time will come when the amount – the output -- will be nearly as large as the input. But now, that is not the case, though, in the future, that will be more increasingly the case. For example, I can't remember the exact name or the correct case for some words. Some I go totally blank on. I get a vague picture of what it is, but it isn't clear enough. I can remember clearly what I had to say to in the first part, but I can't remember a thing just afterwards within the exact same time frame. Two sentences knocking against one another. It is nerve wracking.

Anyhow, this is the phrase or the sentence for now, and the possibility will be that the statements that I make will be longer and have more words in them. But I will also have to slow the process down to remember things as they do come in to my mind, speaking to the <u>thought</u> clearly and accurately so that it comes slowly into the <u>voice</u> just as clearly and accurately. I have so many words to speak now, many more than I had before.

I start out in the early morning with the slowed-down version, but the correct language, the correct version (or pretty much the correct one), and the correct pronunciation of the phrase or sentence. In fact, my day really starts out strong. My day, through the middle part, stays essentially the same, depending on the quality of the sound and the voice, but through the last part of the day there is a decrease in the quality of the word sounds and the vocal chords. I can say the sentence quite clearly in the morning and in the afternoon, but not so clearly as the clock begins to wind down. The words and the vocal chords are tired out, I guess. The last hour or two that I stay awake at night slows down to a nearly zero miles per hour. But I will keep working on it, and it will get better and better!

THE BREATHING SEQUENCE

On my mother's side, my grandfather, Ralph, brought me down to swim with him in Lake Ontario. He had six grandsons, and I was the first one. The water, near Bronte, Canada, was frigid. I was about eight or nine months old, and I "swam" around before I could walk. I swam for more than 75 years, and I didn't even think about it. So the right arm, the right breathing stroke, and the right leg were all "prepped" for the test. This test was to determine whether I could swim at all after the stroke. I could do all four swimming strokes before the stroke: the crawl stroke, the breaststroke, the backstroke, and the butterfly stroke. I didn't know whether my strength and stamina would be up now for swimming or not. But I had to try and do it!

It was about eighteen months later, and, after the two strokes, I slowly began to swim again. So for the first time, the right arm, the right breathing stroke (rather than the left breathing stroke), and the right leg entered the water sequentially. Each entered the water slightly apart, with the arm coming first, the breathing next, and the leg the last. For the right breathing, I would push out and then pull my arm back until it left the water up as straight as I could hold it. As the arm straightened out, as much as I could possibly make it, I then would place it back into the water again and on out to its full extent. I carried the hand out to the end, as far as I was able, and straightened the arm out to its fullest extent and then to held the arm down as it enters the water. It looks like a "v" approaching, then it turns into an "I" in passing. It was a 90-yard pool, but I could do only swim halfway to the other end of the pool; then I had to rest.

The breathing is the next element to tackle. I didn't see this before now, but the breathing up and down is, in fact, the larger issue. Here is how it is supposed to work. With a normal intake of oxygen, you breathe in above the water and out below the water. However, when you breathe in above the surface of the water and breathe out below the surface of the water, it really does matter what your breathing in and breathing out is like and how you do it. You need to watch the oxygen you take in above the surface of the water and what you put out beneath the surface of the water. It matters a great deal how you take the water in and how you breathe it out!

You need to breath in the oxygen above the water, and then breathe out the same amount below the water. While swimming, your mouth should be held in the proper oval shape when the breathing is fine. But the shape of my mouth was abnormal, in that the breath I took in does not equal the breath I blew out. It requires constant monitoring. With the shape of the mouth looking normal, you will be breathing in above the water and breathing out below the water. Otherwise, you will be breathing oxygen in, and, when you breathe out below the water, you will have gagging problems if you are not constantly alert. Coughing above the surface and gagging beneath the surface constitutes the heart of the problem. So, as I've come to understand it now, I've learned to repursue the problem of breathing in and breathing out. Also, with the constant motion to regulate the passage of breathing in and breathing out, I had to also coordinate the right arm and the right leg. It is a big problem, but not an insurmountable problem.

The last component is the right leg. Two legs are required for swimming, but my right leg is the one at issue. It does have to respond consecutively with the other leg on the left side. The right leg is becoming relatively steadier, but that is what the issue is. My right leg does not kick quite like the one on the left side. The left leg is smoother, but I'm working on it. The right leg is gaining slowly, but the leg is still moving more slowly than the one on the left side.

This is the test: the right arm, the right-hand breathing, and the right leg. And the lesson continues to develop between the arm, the breathing, and the leg. My arm and my leg have come a long way, strengthening as the overall window between the arm and the leg strengthens. The breathing will come along too, but it's moving more slowly. I can feel the arm and the leg are gradually increasing in strength. Breathing in and breathing out is better as well. The coordination is better, too.

The right arm stroke slowly gets quicker, but it is not perfect. I'll wait and see how the right arm matches, in equal strokes, with the left arm. More than anything else, that's what it will take to make them equal. It will take some time, but it won't be too long before the strokes on the right side and on the left side equal out. Every day, it's far more possible that I can grow to control the breathing in relation to the right arm and right leg. Every part is different, but it's also all the same in the framed picture: right arm first, right breathing next, and right leg last. Then the left arm and the left leg, no breathing involved, and then the right arm, the breathing, and the right leg. All the pieces are coming together, and every part is progressively sounder!

PART IV
ROAD TO HEALING

"So here I am, some two and a half years after the stroke. The stroke gave me what I was looking for that day . . . it gave me the ending for the book. It gave me an encounter with the kind of physical suffering that often accompanies aging; it gave me a brush with death; it gave me then the first-hand experience I was lacking back then. I can write about aging now. Having the point of view of a stroke survivor, having come through a catastrophic physical event, I can write about aging in a way I couldn't have before."

Ram Dass, <u>Still Here: Embracing Aging, Changing, And Dying</u>

*   *   *   *   *   *   *   *   *

LEARNING TO SPEAK AGAIN

I was discharged from the hospital, and it was about four or five weeks later when I was "present" for the first class session that met in Amy's, the speech therapist, small office. I also took the two other courses in occupational therapy and physical therapy. All three were helpful for me, but Amy's was the most helpful in every way: coming to class, sitting and waiting for the class, attending the class, and going home from class.

I had the class on Monday and on Thursday mornings. With Amy, the first class and the second class went by so fast that I wasn't prepared for <u>any</u> of the following speech therapy classes. Actually, for the first two months or so, I was both totally unprepared for classes and also totally prepared for classes: both what I wanted to say but didn't quite say, and what I didn't say but wanted to. In both classes, I was silent! I was absolutely frustrated and very sad at the same time. I knew what I wanted to express, but I lacked the language altogether. I did quit periodically, actually practically every week, but Jo didn't! She hung in there, and she kept me going to the end of the sessions.

For the first two months of classes that took place between Amy and me, I had no knowledge, skill, or ability in manufacturing text or responding to text, spoken or written. Also, I couldn't talk much at all to express my response to the sessions. I said a few things, but not many. I could think about some of them but not say the words to express my intention or my meaning at all.

Actually, it took me about two months to catch up to the point that I could see what the sequence was asking me for, in responding to the in-class sessions and for responding to the out-of-class sessions. At times the flow was moving along quite clearly and in a direction I could anticipate and follow along with. Sometimes, though, the flow was totally bewildering. I didn't know where it was going at all. I couldn't figure out what was going on. What to answer, what to say, or how to say it, and yet, all of a sudden, in the next breathe, I could speak clearly, though just for a few short seconds or a minute. And then I couldn't speak again for a few minutes. Suddenly I could speak, and suddenly I couldn't speak.

After a while, Amy said that she would be ready for me to send her in advance what I had prepared for us to focus on in the in-class sessions. I "registered" my acceptance for it, but I wasn't quite ready for sending her the sequences in advance for her comments in class. However, it was just a little later -- a week or so -- that I began to send them off to her. With trepidation, I sent them out to see what would happen to them! For the next three and a half months, she sent me the homework assignments to my e-mail, and, when I had "completed" them, I sent them back to her, also using my e-mail. You will see what I had to do until the end of the course (late August 2010), when I walked away from the final session with her. I could have come back, but I didn't. I carried on without Amy. I went to a few meetings, but I had already surpassed them.

Down the road a while, I have so many words to speak now, many more than I had before. Sometimes they come along flowing smoothly, leading into a longer conversation, and, finally, making a difference to my life and to the people I am with. I can confidently begin a sentence, but then, suddenly, I am blank inside at the second "section" where, just a second ago, I thought I had remembered the whole sequence. Sometimes I remember the whole statement, and sometimes, I think can go on, but I can't. One time I waited for the sentence to unfold, and it was completed. The next time I waited for the sentence to unfold, and it was blank at the end. Maybe I'll always wonder if the sentence is going to be complete or not. Maybe that is where the <u>expressive</u> <u>aphasia</u> is triggered, and it sets in instantly. One time I remember, and the next time I don't. Maybe, the <u>expressive</u> aphasia is a gradually lessening condition. But the <u>aphasia</u> continues: not gone, but one that is diminishing, and one that has the writing better than the speaking.

However, now back at the starting gate, about five months along after I had started speech therapy, I did my first piece for Amy. I have transcribed the e-mails exactly as I wrote them. For four months, Amy mailed her assignments from her workbook to my computer. Once I had a chance to respond, I e-mailed them back to her. Here is what I wrote on my first attempt to complete the sentences on my own, rather than under her direct gaze.

From: Robert P Parker   May 26, 2010   1:01 p.m.
Subject: new message
To: Amy

Amy,
Here are the first two of the two-line menus. See what you can do with them.
1) A book is comprised with two cloth covers, and inside of the book is fair to mid-size (occasionally large) staff of pages. A newspaper is filled a large, soft pages and is designed to be thrown away.
2) To make fresh orange juice, you take a fresh orange (or oranges), squeeze it to dry, and pour it in a fresh glass.
Ready . . .
Bob

Here are the second and third "pieces:"

From: Robert P Parker   May 28, 2010   9:20 p.m.
Response: Re(2): new message
To: Amy

OK. Amy –
2) Ice can be made from a pure vanilla shake or huge tun of ice; water can be made from a slurpy soda or great walls of water. Either way can be fine.

2) You will need to turn on the gas; turn up the cooking gas; turn up the meal to warm it straith through; and serve your master with the veritable fresh hamburger and the fresh roll that came with it.

OK, here's the show for two . . .

Bob

From: Robert P Parker   June 2, 2010   11:25 a.m.
Subject: new message
To: Amy

Amy,

OK, here it goes . . .

1) Bicyclists, despite the noise caused by the suspension, rode up the first, second, a third and a fourth into the free ride. Motorcycle, for a great ride and a good feel, takes off for the coast or mountain.

2) To brush your teeth, you need to grab the brush, keep the brush in hand with the scurrying, and then rinse thoroughly for the next time.

I haven't yet had time to view them . . .

Bob

Here is the fourth "piece:"

From: Robert P Parker   June 16, 2010   9:15 p.m.
Subject: Re(2): new message
To: Amy

Amy,

Here's the damage . . .

3) When you check the level of grass have raised, you have to see the grass is over green. I have to make that determination. Then, you can cut the grass. Mow it; gather up the folds; and make a fine tone.

Here's the next damage.

4) Write a poem: visualize a memory, remember the memory – and shout it out for everyone to hear about. Write a story:

think the story out before you act it out; act it out; then play it out – and wait it is still happening.

OK, here's the damage.

Bob

Here is the fifth "piece:"

From: Robert P Parker   June 26, 2010   9:38 p.m.
Subject: message
To: Amy

Amy,

Here's an "apartment building/office building" . . .

7) The apartment building was built to hold many people. This place could hold more with a pool. The office building was built to hold workers. The place to build office buildings is in a city.

Here's the "beat the eggs" . . .

8) First, you need to a give these eggs a good scramble. Second, you need to give them the essencial of almost-hard. Third, you to give a good waft of scramble egg at the end.

First, you need to take this . . .

Bob

Here are the sixth and seventh "pieces," plus the only one that Amy responded to. She gave her responses during the in-class session.

From: Robert P Parker   June 27, 2010   8:09 p.m.
Subject: Re(6): new message
To: Amy

Amy,

Here's the "make oatmeal" one . . .

9) To make oatmeal, you must make a good one. You have to take oatmeal, drizzle it in the pot of hot water until it becomes thick, and nurse it along until the soup is created ready to go.

Well, guess I don't have much . . .
Bob

From: Robert P Parker   July 1, 2010 7:50 p.m.
Subject: Re(7): new message
To: Amy

Amy,
I have it.
    5) To make good oatmeal, you have to make it by measuring and by taking the results of the measure. Then, you periodically boil water, add the oatmeal, and stir.
How do you like it now?
Bob

From: Amy   July 1, 2010 8:16 p.m.
Subject: RE: new message
To: Robert P Parker

"Much better. Here's my correction."
    6) To make good oatmeal, you have to make it by measuring **the oatmeal** and by taking the results of the measure and measure water. (?) Then, you periodically boil water, add the oatmeal, and stir.
"What do you think? We'll talk on Tuesday. Have a good weekend."
Amy

Here is the eighth "piece." I think this is where the whole thing begins to come together a little bit more than beforehand. Look carefully at this one in particular, and then read the next few pieces in a sequence. You will see a gain from here on.

From: Robert P Parker   July 5, 2010 5:04 p.m.
Subject: new message
To: Amy

Amy,
"Clean the living room"? OK . . .

10) I don't clean the living room. The cleaning lady cleans it. She makes a living cleaning it. Why would I do that? I've completely forgotten how to do it.

"coal/oil"? OK . . .

11) Coal is black, but the major difference is coal is solid. Oil is liquid, and it is used for heat.

Bob

Here is the ninth "piece:"

From: Robert P Parker   July 7, 2010   10:42 p.m.
Subject: another new message
To: Amy

Amy,
Wow, I "make a good cup of coffee"!

12) I want to make good coffee. I start with the beans into the coffee grinder. I pour the water, put the one teaspoonful to a cup, turn on the appropriate burner, and wait for the first cup to be finished.

Ouch, watch the "iron/steel"?

13) Iron ore is from one source; steel is from many sources. Iron is from one strength; steel has multiple uses.

Bob

Here is the tenth "piece:"

From: Robert P Parker   July 21, 2010   8:09 p.m.
Subject: Re: Fwd: another(!) new message(s)
To: Amy

Amy,

18) The eyes bring in the warmth and blessing of visibility. The ears bring in the earthy tones of viability.

19) Fans generate cooling downward; heater generates heating upwards.

20) Teacher teaches a lesson to a student; the student really studies the lesson as hard as she could.

They're finished!

Bob

Here is the eleventh "piece:"

From: Robert P Parker   July 21, 2010   8:47 p.m.
Subject: new messages
To: Amy

Amy,
1)   Coffee is a great way to the start day. We go to the Jones house to get our cappuccino.
2)   Apple is a fruit. Apples come in so many colors and so many flavors.
3)   Thee purpose of the pen is the used to write with.
4)   I used the knife to cut the bread.
5)   I read the book by one day and one half. Ain't that a wrip!

Bob

And here is the final one:

From: Robert P Parker   August 16, 2010   11:07 a.m.
Subject: messages
To: Amy

Amy,
Here's another riff . . .
1)   Someone hit my car this morning. I took it in stride.
2)   When I wear the heart on my sleeve, everyone knows it.
3)   I raised the bet to $50 and didn't bat an eyelash.
4)   When I'm talking to someone else, he always puts his two cents in.
5)   I certainly raised the tip of the iceberg during the morning.

Bob

I give thanks to Amy, to Jo, and to the people in my life who are patient and allow me to speak. I've made some real progress with all of them. I will be all right on my own. But, three years from now, I will still be trying to put together sentences that work. I imagine these sentences, however, to be even longer, better shaped, and richer in content than the ones that have been previously produced.

PART V
INCREASING MOMENTS OF UNDERSTANDING

"Everything that has been made from love is alive."

Anne Michaels, <u>The Winter's Vault</u>, 2009

* * * * * * * * *

CHALLENGES AND INNER RESOURCES

This book is about <u>being</u> healed and <u>approaching</u> wellness. Over four years that I have begun to write and to speak again, my writing ability is now at 85%, and the speaking ability is at 60%. Also my right arm and hand are 75%. But it did not start out that way. The writing and the speaking were at ground zero, and the right arm, the hand, and the fingers were at ground zero. The right leg was 60%. But, and this is the big "but," the voice, the arm, the hand, the fingers, and right leg are working hard at getting better all the time. I've also lost 65 pounds! I started out at 222 pounds, and I ended up at 157 pounds. I look a lot slimmer and fitter. Plus, my colleagues say that I look younger. I don't know about that, but other people tell me I'm looking more youthful. So, I've made a complete shift in focus: in mind and in body. I'm acting differently: by intention and by commitment. And I'm still not finished improving yet.

INCAPACITATED

Being incapacitated was the lowest rung. I hit the bottom. There was no way that I could do anything for myself. It was totally in Jo's hands. I was lying flat on my back with no feeling in my right arm and hand. In addition, I had expressive aphasia. I "knew" only five noises, not even sounds let alone words! I had to learn the whole language again! Also, after about two weeks during which I had been totally incapacitated, I had to get up and start to relearn the legs with walking slowly step by step: two nurses, one on each side, and the one nurse had to hold onto my ties to make sure that I wouldn't fall over. My arm, too, was literally dead, and I had to put it in a sling. Confined wouldn't capture it! I was completely reliant on other people.

But I, actually we, <u>had</u> to get started. I felt helpless, but not hopeless. Not the idea of overcoming it, but the idea the leadership, and the will to succeed with Jo and others who were walking step-by-step close to me. So, I started: one step ahead and one step back, then two steps ahead and one step back. You know, mini-steps, but they were huge steps to me and to Jo. I took them slowly but steadily in the direction that I wanted to go so that the healing slowly took me to the top.

CONFINEMENT

The next phase was confinement. Early on, when I finally did sit up by <u>myself</u>, not the nurses holding me up, Jo and the nurses watched, and I did not stumble or take a fall. I moved infinitesimally slowly, but I was sitting up <u>by myself</u>, two legs over the side of the bed. Then, I stood up by <u>myself</u> to my full height, one hand hanging onto the bed and the other hanging limply in the sling. I don't know how I did it, but I did it. Then, with one hand holding onto the wheelchair, I moved one or two shuffling steps to the wheelchair by <u>myself</u>! Then I sat down again, not in the bed but in the wheelchair! I was exhausted, out of breath, but I had made it to the wheelchair. I had made it out of bed, two steps to the wheelchair with the left hand holding on for dear life, and down into wheelchair, by myself! Jo and the nurses were watching again like hawks, but I didn't stumble or fall no matter how slowly or how gingerly I moved! So I was taken around the room, not by the bed but in the wheelchair.

Later, I stood for a few minutes and with the nurse standing by to catch me if I fell over or passed out. I then tried my hand at shaving for the first time. I shaved very slowly and gingerly with my left hand, but it worked. It was another "big" experience, although I can't remember exactly what happened immediately afterward!

Or in another setting, one of us seated right here with the wheelchair on my side of the table and Amy seated on the other side of the table. I sat for my third or fourth session with her, and, after two or three times of the session, I could now <u>try</u> to sound out the letter "I" to Amy. I tried and tried, and now, all of a sudden, I <u>finally</u> made it to pronounce the "I." It doesn't seem like much now, but I worked the whole session to pronounce the word "I." The next session, I could then sound out the letters to "I could," and it took the whole session to do that one thing. In the next session, I could now pronounce the words "I could not." Now I had three words to begin the sentence, but not one word to end the sentence.

DETERMINATION

The third phase was determination. I have experienced that up close and personal: the things that I have learned to do for myself that I could not do just two or three months ago. For example, I couldn't see how the right fingers would make the hand work when it zips up the jacket. So, just when I thought I had it on, the zipper slipped back off again. I almost had it, but not quite. So I asked Jo for help. The first part was done because Jo made the zipper work, and up it went for an inch or two. Then I took hold again to move the zipper up to the top, but the zipper wouldn't quite make it halfway to the top. The zipper didn't do quite what I wanted it to do. So, in that instance, I needed Jo's help again, to roll the zipper up to the top of the jacket. Jo had zipped, in effect, the whole jacket up, right from the beginning to the end.

Or, here's another example. This one started out as confinement but made its way to determination. I simply couldn't put on my blue jeans by myself. I had to get hold of my right pant's leg, any way I could, and put it on. Now, I had to get a hold of my left pant's leg, and, you're right, I did it mostly with Jo's help. Also, Jo started it out by zipping the fly for me, and then, when I got hold of that part of the operation, I started doing it more and more for myself. And, eventually, I had to make it to the place where I could put the pants on by <u>myself</u> entirely. Actually, it was a long series of steps from confinement toward determination. It was much slower than I thought it would be, but I will slowly increase the speed and flexibility.

SELF-DETERMINATION

The fourth phase was self-determination: that is the main goal I am aiming toward. But, here is where I am at this point: half determination, with someone else participating in it, and then moving toward whole self-determination, where no one else is participating in it. I'm pretty good about not going to another person to get a phrase for what I want to say, but sometimes I can't make it through to end of the sentence. So I have to borrow a word or words from one of them. Ah, that is the right word, and I'll put the words out as "my" speaking to someone else! The word comes "from" their mouth, but, putting it in as the last part of the sentence I utter, it is "mine," too. I mean, it is all right to do this, to add a "switch" in the words, but I would like it better that they came from my own "head" instead of from a partner in the dialogue. He or she freely gives it to me, but still, I can't speak it until I hear the word, realize it's the right word (or more or less the right word), and then speak it out loud for myself and for my colleagues.

The writing has progressed further than I can speak, either fluently or intelligently. Not input, which is fine, but output. For example, I can pronounce the word "alphabetically", but in my "mind." There is no problem when I pronounce it silently. But I can only speak the word "al – pha – bet – ic – al – ly", and I don't get it right until the second or third try! I can pronounce them all internally, but not externally. But I am able now to speak them aloud as sentences and paragraphs, but slowly, gradually, and intermittently. So, the writing has definitely moved further than the speaking, but the speaking is coming along, too.

SIX SMALL GOALS

My arm (elbow, wrist, and fingers), thanks to Tai Chi, swimming, and treadmill, is better as well. I now can practice self-determination to aim for six small goals. For example, brushing my teeth, or shaving and showering, or doing a load of wash (whether hot or cold), or hanging up my t-shirts, taking them down and putting them away, or changing the bed by myself, or washing the dishes and putting them away by myself: all of these are approaching <u>independence</u>. I'm not there yet, but I'm getting better at it in the different varieties of actions that I can now take on.

INDEPENDENCE

The final goal is independence. Either way, we can make it separately, independently, or we make it together as part of a collaborative effort. But that goal lies ahead, though not too far ahead. So I will wait and see whether I can read, listen, write, speak, listen to classical and jazz music, do Tai Chi, swim, and do an increasing amount of housework even better than I do now. I can see it more clearly than ever. It is just a bit further on from here, but I can make it. It is a rapidly approaching healing and wellness!

This has been the start of things for me and for Jo, and we will be pushing on toward the end of the book. I know that I will make some of it happen, or, perhaps, all of it will happen. And I know that you will make it happen, too! It may take you longer than you want, but **<u>you and I</u> can make it happen regardless of how long it takes!**

ACKNOWLEDGMENTS

To my doctors, I wish to express my deepest and heartfelt thanks to each of you: Arbi Ohanion, MD; Michael Gurevitch, MD; Paulette Saddler, MD; Ashish Patel, MD; Roy S Kohl, Jr, MD; Yafa Minazad, MD; Azhil Durairaj, MD.

To Barbara Miller, my editor, who willingly and patiently agreed to work with me. She wanted to know whether I could change the book fairly radically, or whether it could stand on its own. I said, "By all means, let's go for it!" and so she began to work on revamping and reorganizing the entire book: from the Preface to Part I through the Acknowledgments to the Appendices. Because of my speech problems, the work was slow but steady, but Barbara hung in there with me.

To all my friends and family who came to visit me in the hospital, who came to visit when I returned home, who called or sent cards and drawings of encouragement, who walked and talked with me, who supported Jo in the myriad chores she had to do with me, and so much more. I've chosen not to name names because I know I would leave someone out, but I know who you are. Thank you from the bottom of my heart!

APPENDIX I

SOCIAL INTERACTIONS

I learned more from social interaction than in any other way. I listened to it, learned from it, and gradually, more and more, participated in it. People talked with me, walked with me, and, generally, helped me out when I was stuck on a word. Everyone was a participant. That was the start of it.

The voices and the warmth: I might get a word in now and then, but that's all I was capable of doing. It was listening to me or talking with me. But, over time and as a result, I had gradually more words to use and a wider variety of situations to use them in. Consequently, I got gradually better at using them. For instance, a person told me about the book I was reading, or the show I was watching. I could understand all of it. But then, they waited for me to try to speak back to them, at least as much I could, but, slowly, it got better also. That is where we spent the bulk of our time together. We carried on the dialogue that made it real, exciting, and fun. But, as I participated more, it made me more hopeful!

JONES COFFEE ROASTERS

Soon after I was discharged from the hospital, I rejoined the Jones Coffee Roasters for the social interaction and the cappuccinos. I can recall going in there the first time, with Jo, and proudly holding the arm barely one-third above the level of the cash register. However, it was zero a week ago, when I couldn't move it at all. I also garbled the words "Thank you" to the baristas. One day it came out sort of fine, and the next day it came out totally muddled. But it was just the phrase "Thank you" that they cared about. Mrs. Jones always came over to ask how I was doing. Each of the baristas checked in with me. They, and Mrs. Jones, just wanted to see me getting better all the time.

After about a month the Roasters moved down the street. Sometimes Jo was here, and sometimes she was at the pulmonary rehabilitation unit. The baristas always made me and Jo feel welcome. Overtime we became one of the regulars. I was immediately included in their gathering, and it didn't matter how little I spoke at that point. I learned how to take things in, and slowly turn them around to make them go out again as spoken words. It was painfully slow, but I learned.

SAMBALATTE

In April 2011, we moved back from Pasadena to Las Vegas. I loved the new coffee shop called Sambalatte. Don and Sally were so surprised to see Jo and I in Sambalattte, so soon after we arrived back in town. Don and Luiz had agreed to start the business from scratch: Don with the roasted beans and Luiz with the coffee, tea, pastries, and sandwiches.

These people are friends. I can't tell you how much I have advanced through the "sessions" with them. I had to use words that I hadn't used at all since the stroke. I had to "summon them" into my speech in a hurry. Perhaps I "shuffled" them over from my interior conversation to an external conversation called speaking. I don't know what the "source" is, although maybe the source is "switching" things back and fourth between the input to the output and back to the input again.

I used "them" to make a comment, or a point, or to ask a question, or to express satisfaction, or to register confusion. Most of the time, the person "got" the intended comment, more or less, and I responded to his continuing conversation. If she didn't, she asked me a question: say, "Hold it. Wait a minute. I don't understand that word (or words)." We could then straighten out the word or words, and then the conversation would continue as normal. There would be a part where I would speak, and then he/she would speak too – an ordinary conversation!

These women and men entered into a conversation with me, one with depth, substance, and good humor. I, really we, explored the area together. For me, the beginnings of elegance and lucidity began to show up in my writing particularly but also in my speaking. I grew to love everyone who involved him or herself in the conversation with me and with Jo.

APPENDIX II

AN EXCITING TEACHING CHALLENGE

In my 49th year, I was teaching doctoral students at the University of La Verne (La Verne, CA). I was assigned to reorganize the new, radically revised, two-year doctoral research curriculum, and it was totally in my hands to do what I wanted with it! I found it a fantastic year to think inside, all alone with my thoughts, and out loud, with a couple of friends to discuss and to agree to changes in the curriculum. It took me about four or five months to create the new research curriculum. Then, to teach the curriculum, half of it as it turned out, and to continue to revise the curriculum were the next steps in the process.

I had to discard the entire "standard" research program and that was the easy part, but I had the ongoing experience of organizing doctoral students at Rutgers into an entire new set of books and readings for the Year One and Year Two research curriculum, and that was the hardest part. I wanted this new group at La Verne to become a real listening, reading, and writing group, by talking with others in relationships and by growing stronger by leading and following each other across disciplines. In the first semester of Year 1,. The webinars and/or the seminars were arranged in six sessions: Getting Started & Knowing What To Do; The Nature of Theory; The Nature of Inquiry; Questions? The Nature of the Knowing Process; and Developing A Theory & Writing A Theory Paper.

Listening to various other discussants, talking and writing with others, and making their way outside of the individual groups, whether for talking and/or writing, was hard for many of the doctoral students to do. But for other doctoral students, over time, it became increasingly easier for them to do. It was new from the beginning, but they had "picked up" the curriculum. As the theories became clearer, they "sensed," or they actually knew, what they should do with these theories in order to put them into practice. These doctoral students had a feeling, followed by a idea, that if they knew the theory, or at least a part of it anyhow, and they could get started on the rest of the theory. It became clearer that they did know something about the theory. Each doctoral student would have an opportunity to construct a deeper understanding of the nature and function of a theory. Depending on the depth with which he/she understood the theory, as well as an understanding of the inquiry process and a greater knowledge in presenting an extended piece of written discourse, they would have the ability to envision the constructivist perspective in real life terms.

The personal inquiry paper was exciting, too, so that the students could choose among the various theories. They could choose to connect one theory in particular or several theories in general. They could use it as the basis for formulating a metaphor: one theory contrasting with a different theory. It all hinged on what speculations they could produce or derive; what they could gain from the experiences and situations they had; and what the tentative conclusions of that theory (or theories) could be verified.

Regardless, you can develop the piece of writing so that a personal theory emerges; you have tested it; and you can report the results. Based on a theory (or theories) and based on your sense of what represents a good "theory," you can turn it into a logically structured theory of inquiry, and that's what the students did. I told the students, "Your challenge in writing this paper (was) to develop a coherent, logically structured theory of inquiry that integrates the complementary processes into self and self-other relationships." I finished the first half of the seminars, but, in between, I hadn't collected the students' essays yet. I had the stroke on December 22, 2009 at 10:15 a.m.

APPENDIX III

CONVERSATIONS WITH OTHER WRITERS

I reached to friends to get the answers I "wanted," desperate to have them. And I did — and more!

PETER BROWN

I wanted to hear/read more. Wow, what a relief it is to hear <u>my "speaking" voice answering to my "answering" voice</u>! Now they have both become a single entity! Before I desperately wanted to hear the "voice" myself to know what to look for, but I didn't quite know how to ask that fundamental piece about the voice yet! And yet you put the <u>voice</u> first! The voice lays the groundwork and brings them together: what the actual voice sounds like and looks like! And it does reverberate the <u>sound</u> of <u>Bob</u> throughout the book.

Who is doing the asking, and who does the answering? It is the same Bob. It is now possible that the "Bob" who is doing the asking is also the "Bob" for whom I am doing the answering! Before I wasn't so sure! But it is true for "seeing" what the sound of the voice looks like, and it's also true for what the arm looks like and what the hand and the fingers look like. From the voice to the different versions of the whole right side of the body: it does hold all of the "voices" together.

I say 'hear' to focus on the intangible that drove it all for me – your [Bob's] 'voice'. I asked myself if I didn't know you would have the knowledge and the experience and if the voice

will have taken on the same power after the stroke? Maybe not as much as before that stroke – because knowledge of you and your experience really carried a resonance all the way through – but finally, yes. I worked hard on the text to make the knowledge and the voice come out clearly. I couldn't quite be sure then, but it's now coming together. It's before the stroke <u>and</u> after the stroke. I've become "Bob" throughout the stroke! I didn't know how far the knowledge, the experience, and the voice would carry me. I didn't know for sure that the voice would ever show up again. I lost it forever, or at least I thought I had, but then I found it once again! But, evidently, I went even further than I had thought possible. It is now a single voice!

And I do hear 'you' all the way in/through varied aspects of your voice: confidence, despair, resolution, puzzlement . . . Through the voice a full and complex protagonist emerges -- one on a harrowing and intriguing journey. The stuff of a good read. All those verbs, adjectives, and adverbs are struggling to become alive there in the book: a harrowing but intriguing journey for me. I have been putting it together, agonizingly, piece by piece, reshuffling the manuscript, and stepping back to see the entire book.

It is **a setting which flits in and out of the surreal and starkly clinical**. The first time I woke up, post-stroke, I opened my eyes and took in the faces to see who was staring back at me. All the eyes were riveted to mine. It took me a few seconds to register the glances from Jo, to the nurses, over to Jen and Sandy, and then back to me. Just after that, I could "feel" a swing to Jo, then to the nurses, then over to Jen and Sandy, and back to me. I "sensed" that my voice had a roughly half-garbage and half-sane "message" in it. I could hear my voice say a couple of things rationally, and, suddenly, my voice was back to irrational. But after the second stroke, one week later, I had no words at all, just five noises! The voice had closed down.

Or the "starkly clinical": "I immediately met the patient [Parker] in the CT scanner room where he underwent a CT scan as well the CT angiogram and a CT perfusion . . . it was determined that he had a likely watershed infarction, though was less than one-third of middle cerebral artery territory. Also at that time he was noted to have an NIH Stroke Scale of 16, therefore, full-dose t-PA [once only] was initiated at 11:30 am [A. O. MD, 12/22/09]." I was unconscious, but for how long I don't really know: in and out of consciousness. That was about as "starkly clinical" as I could get.

   . . . a**nd language development; forgetting and remembering – memory, which I find to be the matrix of the whole thing. You clearly challenged and used your memory in new ways, used it well, and have acquired important insights into its nature which you might not otherwise have had**. Forgetting and remembering: suddenly a "flash" comes in –- a word or phrase or sentence; I write it down and translate it to the piece of the writing on the computer, correct it, and let it stand for a while. It "sounds" right. But then, I get another "flash", and it "tells" me not to leave the word or phrase in or to move it to another place entirely. Sometimes it "tells" me what to do, and I do it; sometimes it tells me what not to do, and I don't do it, and the word or phrase is just fine as is! I honestly don't know how this "message" works, but it is helpful!

   I "know" that the words, phrases, sentences, and paragraphs will line up just so and in the right order. I can remember the entire line and begin to type it in. Or I can remember the first half, but then I forget the second half of the line. Yet, while I'm typing some words that I can remember, I can't finish the line because the typing is just so slow or because I have clearly forgotten again. I just don't know which was which: slow typing or just do not remembering the second half of the sentence. Gradually, though, I am remembering not just one line, but, actually, two or three lines together! And this is how I build the manuscript: piece by piece, retyping again and again.

   Also, I get better at typing the lines, "reading" it out when I'm finished typing, and typing in the next portion! In fact, I am remembering slightly more all the parts of the message. I can remember even the string of words, in sequence, until the end of a line. I can't remember two strings of words, but I can remember one string of words, even up to the end of the section.

   Point of view – the sense of location is provocative. A car, the ambulance, the gurney, the hospital, flat on my back, expressive aphasia, the right arm, Jo (all 43 consecutive nights!), the nurses, the wheelchair, the bathroom, Amy, and the cane: BUT I'm finally standing on my own, and I am walking around. Yes, the "transitions must have been challenging in their own right", but I have changed all of the voices to make it consistent. I had a fantastic grammar, but

83

it's not like that anymore. You know that I have a smaller vocabulary. Although it is starting to rebuild and to generate more vocabulary, more syntax, and more grammar, I also have a much better "feel" now than I did for vocabulary and grammar.

A really absorbing read and reread. Invites engaged interpretation. Yes, it does indeed "Invite[s] engaged interpretation". It does and at many different levels of the book, too: from the grim beginning to the healing end of the book. And Kay: you can't make this stuff up! Actually, this whole journey just has to be the truth!

I think you're right about the question that plagues all of us: . . . **the continuing evolution of your mind and its language prompts a lot of reflection on 'progress.** What is progress? Is it something that we can move toward, or is it just out of reach? Toward healing? Toward wellness? I have a piece of the answer, but not the whole answer yet.

DEENA LINETT

[I]t is so odd how having a reader makes it possible to see one's own text better. And you can't 'pretend' to have a reader – you have to have a real one! So I'm glad to have performed that function for you. Just the hours you spent reading the book made it real and truthful to me. It also gave me some readers out there something that had to be acknowledged: yes, this is the truth. I know that I can put in a word, phrase, sentence, or paragraph that it makes sense. I hadn't "seen" what the word or phrase said before, but now I can see it clearly. You have made me be more specific about that sentence or paragraph which I had overlooked.

I think subheads or head-notes, and some identifying information will be a great help to orient and locate the reader. I started in the same day that I received your e-mail! I wrote head-notes and/or subheads right from the beginning of the book. They were an incredible addition to the manuscript. I also added some identifying information about the speech therapist (Amy), the good friends (Mark and others), my daughter (Jen) and my son-in-law (Sandy), and my brother, Steve. I also made it double-spaced throughout the book.

I very much like the small pieces; they're sort of like a jig-saw puzzle, but not puzzling. I agree with that notion: the writing is smaller than it was before, really two or three pages at the longest stretch. But, also, it is as tight as I can make it, and it's easy to read. I don't think you'll have much trouble at all when you put them in a row, in a "jig-saw" puzzle, because I think it's "not puzzling."

I found the manuscript easy to read and to follow and . . . (also) brave, moving, and often beautiful. Thank you for those wonderful comments! You found it matched the "brave, moving, and often beautiful."

Brave: I felt totally wasted, totally blasted – the worst news of all that I could possibly imagine was being without language. No language: I could not go any further down. That was it! I just couldn't imagine re-learning that language again! Yet, I did once again re-learn English, and I am still doing it! I had to be "brave" to make it as far as I've come!

Moving: For a period of time the wheelchair was sufficient, but then, when I stood erect, even for a moment, supported by nurses, I asked for a brief period, free for a second or two, for me to walk without holding onto anything else except the wall and the cane. So, on my feet, I held on to the wall and the cane, then, later, I held on to the cane! I was standing alone with nothing but the cane: all alone, no hands on anything else, holding onto nothing except for the cane. Then, I moved just a bit, but I did move! It worked!" So, I have continued to do make these moves gradually, over two years and a half, and I'm still doing it now: in Tai Chi (three times per week), swimming (two time week), treadmill (twice per week), writing, reading, and music, and the other kinds of exercises. I had to "re-move" again to develop for me, for Jo, and for the other friends all over the place the sense that I could do it!.

Often Beautiful: So, the pressure is on, to move slowly but steadily to increase my capacity to a be a participant in a conversation, made in a light, bantering tone or a deep, serious tone. Five minutes is not the issue. It's more like a pull for me to become a full participant in a conversation. Nothing out of the ordinary, but in a conversation that continues for some time with the participants in it . . . I can see the progress over the past few months. Slowly, I'm in the process of getting better and better at it all of the time. Yes, you're right! I am getting better at it, but it is slow, gradual, but a hopeful stance to take, especially toward the future!

And more: **You never sound self-pitying or in any way unappealing. In fact, I thought several times I could hear your voice, the Bob I know, and the warmth in your voice.** Yes, I finally heard my own voice break through! You're right: I never have sounded "self-pitying." It is a hopeful book.

The only thing I didn't do was to **add some sensuous details: color, scent, textures, voices** – for example, the coffee is <u>smooth or frothy</u>! But I still haven't been able to do anything with any of the "sensuous details". I'm struggling with it, but it will come eventually.

CONTENTS

American Stroke Association, 2014, n.d (website).

Dass, Ram, <u>Embracing Aging, Changing, and Dying</u>. New York,,2000.

Didion, Joan. <u>Blue Nights</u>. New York, Alfred A. Knopf, 2011.

Evans, Robert. <u>The Fat Lady Sang</u>. HarperCollinsPublisher/itbooks, 2013.

Michaels, Anne. <u>The Winters Vault</u>. Toronto, McClelland & Stewart, 2009.

Toibin, Colm. <u>Brooklyn</u>.

Printed in the United States
By Bookmasters